THE

MBA

CAREER

MOVING ON THE FAST TRACK TO SUCCESS

by
Eugene Bronstein
and
Robert D. Hisrich

Professors of Marketing
School of Management
Boston College

Barron's Educational Series, Inc.
Woodbury, New York ● London ● Toronto ● Sydney

All inquiries should be addressed to:
Barron's Educational Series, Inc.
113 Crossways Park Drive
Woodbury, New York 11797

Library of Congress Catalog Card No. 82-18478
International Standard Book No. 0-8120-2485-0

Library of Congress Cataloging in Publication Data
Bronstein, Eugene, 1925–
    The MBA career.

    1. Executives—Vocational guidance—United States.
2. Master of business administration degree—
United States.   I. Hisrich, Robert D.   II. Title.
HF5500.3.U54B73   1982   685.4'09   82-18478
ISBN 0-8120-2485-0

PRINTED IN THE UNITED STATES OF AMERICA
345   800   9876543

Contents

Introduction

$\mathbf{W}$hat is this all about? It is about getting from here to there, from now to then. It is about planning, then realizing a successful and rewarding career as a manager. While alone this book is static, your input makes a creative and active process evolve. The concepts and strategies introduced here will help you launch your career as an MBA or make the transition into a new management position if you are already employed. Once learned and practiced, these concepts and strategies—along with your personal experience and academic attributes—will provide a solid foundation for your growth and success as a manager.

Underlying the discussions in this book is the view of the MBA as a professional—as a decision-maker who is a creative thinker and problem solver and who deals with ideas as well as people. In addition, the MBA has the ability to communicate well, take risks, and convey an enthusiasm for business processes and ethics.

Whether you are going to graduate this year or are switching from one area in management to another, you will have to work hard. Obtaining an optimal position is an art. Once learned, it can be used whenever necessary. You will change jobs and probably careers several times during your lifetime, and a series of company and job changes is the norm. By planning on a long-term basis you have a good framework for intelligent change. Although you are probably concerned about getting a first job, you will have more long-term options if you plan correctly. All the work you do now will make it that much easier later on.

Throughout the process of launching a career, keep in mind two things. First, it is often a lonely and painful process; there will be times when you feel depressed and frightened, but this is normal and has been felt by most MBAs. Second, remember that no one person has the complete answer for you and your career; you need yourself to answer many of the personal questions, plus you should utilize other resources mentioned frequently throughout the book.

Many people—business executives, editors, professors, and students—have contributed to this book. While they are too numerous to mention individually where appropriate, they are acknowledged in footnotes and other references throughout the book. We are especially indebted to the project editor, Carole Berglie; to our research assistant, Nancy Hansen, for her editorial assistance; to Fay Bronstein and Chris Merkle in helping to develop Chapter 1; and to Nicola Argerake, Jerrie Redding, and Anne Shenkman for typing various portions of the manuscript.

This book is dedicated to our loving wives, Fay and Tina, and children, Dave, Fred, Jeff, Kary, Katy, and Kelly, whose support and understanding made this effort possible.

1

The Psychology
of the
Job Campaign

In this age of self-awareness it is important to feel good about ourselves. Self-confidence and self-esteem, though intangible, profoundly influence actions and behavior throughout a person's life. The period of the job hunt is no exception. Your amount of self-confidence and self-esteem are evident in matters small and large. Establishing eye contact, extending a hand in greeting, walking into a room in a certain manner—ordinary gestures such as these provide a potential employer with telling clues about your self-perception. If you feel confident, then your behavior mirrors that confidence. Your emotional state of mind reflects itself in other, more subtle ways as well. It dictates your approach to the process of finding a job and the effectiveness of your strategy. Perhaps most importantly, it helps you weather the mounting tension and stress produced by the job hunt itself.

Job hunting can be a very stressful, tension-ridden experience, evoking fear, anxieties, and anger—painful feelings which create self-doubt and nagging ambivalence, erode confidence, and sap energy. Over time these symptoms of distress can seriously impede the progress of your search, unless you truly learn to understand and recognize your symptoms and learn also to cope with them.

The objective of this first chapter is to examine the stresses that invariably accompany the job search and to suggest some very practical ways of dealing with them. We are convinced that good mental health is fundamental to the success of finding a job and provides the really solid underpinnings that will carry you through the months of your campaign. The information and insights in this chapter will lay the foundation for the development and implementation of a productive and successful strategy, the aspects of which are discussed in the remaining chapters of this book.

None of us is a stranger to anxiety and fear. Think about your feelings as you embark on a new venture. Even a pleasant vacation miles away from the familiarity of your home can provoke a tinge of anxiety. While you may refer to these feelings as "butterflies" in your stomach, actually they are symptoms of your anxiety in the face of the unknown.

The job hunt is riddled with unknowns. While there are a number of strategies for reducing unknown elements, nevertheless every time you pick up the telephone or walk into an interview you are faced with the unknown in the guise of a new and strange face in an unfamiliar context.

Perhaps the best way to illustrate this state of anxiety is to relate the job search of Jennifer, who at age 24 had completed an MBA program with a concentration in marketing. Jennifer had received an undergraduate degree in English and had entered the MBA program directly upon completion of her undergraduate degree without obtaining any business background. She began the job search with considerable anxiety. To her the business world was a complete mystery, an unknown entity. Her fears were reinforced when she discovered in the course of her job search that most of the openings were in sales rather than product management, her major area of interest. Here is the substance of her thoughts: "What do I know about sales? In fact, what do I know about business? The only thing I've ever done is read textbooks and write term papers. I know absolutely nothing about the business world. This MBA program didn't train me for sales . . . maybe I should go after a more traditional job . . . maybe I should forget about business and go back to school for a master's degree in English. I don't know if I really want to compete in the business world."

Jennifer's fears about the unknown had seriously muddled her logical thought processes, creating self-doubts and negative feelings about her worth before she had really tested the saleability of her skills in the marketplace. Jennifer's anxieties about the unknown were bound up with common fears about performance and evaluation. Do you remember how you felt when you received your first report card or the grade on your first college term paper? Or when you made your first public speech? The signs of anxiety were unmistakable: a churning stomach, an aching head, sweaty hands, a racing pulse. Most people worry about performing and measuring up, especially if they are being judged by others. Even theatrical and musical personalities admit to stage fright before their performances.

One aspect of the job search—the interview process—scrutinizes the candidate's performance with a question-and-answer format designed to elicit information and insight which will be helpful in the decision-making process. Sometimes a potential employer will interview a candidate two or three times, evaluating strengths and weaknesses, skills and experiences before reaching a final decision. Sometimes a performance on a single day will affect the outcome. Small wonder that MBAs display anxiety symptoms in the face of this psychologically rigorous experience. The details of the interview process, and some of the steps that can be taken to minimize this stress, are discussed in Chapter 8. At best, interviews are nerve-wracking. If MBAs recognize this fact, then they are on their way to dealing with the many stresses encountered.

MBA graduates in the job marketplace also often suffer from additional anxieties, created by high and sometimes unrealistic expectations which they have for themselves and which have been thrust upon them by their school, faculty, peers, and family.

John's story is a case in point. John worked in the nonprofit sector for five years before entering the MBA program at a very prestigious school, majoring in financial analysis. He began the job hunt with the unshakable conviction that his degree would automatically open the doors of industry, prompting countless job offers for a middle-management position as an assistant comptroller, even though he had had no previous business experience in financial analysis. He was so sure of instant success that he actually skipped the very important procedure of informational interviewing, an extremely important link in the job-strategy chain which is discussed in Chapter 4. A concern for his image and anxiety about not living up to the school's expectations pushed John to set up unrealistic goals for himself. Six months passed without a single job offer; John never got past the first round of interviews. His anxiety about living up to expectations had truly impeded his job search. When he finally realized that he would not qualify for a middle-level management position, he readjusted his sights and accepted an entry-level position in a training program for comptrollers.

Don is another example of a candidate under pressure. At thirty-five, Don—married, with two children—enrolled in an MBA evening program to help him make the leap from middle to upper management. Don had taken his family members into his confidence, and they had approved his return to school even though it meant considerable sacrifice, both in terms of money and in the quality of their family life. Under heavy tension, Don started to look for a job. He worried about not meeting his professional objective and disappointing his family, who had remained loyal and supportive through the years of his education. He had other concerns as well. He wondered about his ability to make the adjustment to another business company as well as leaving fellow workers. Since he might even be forced to make a geographical move in order to widen his options, he was concerned about his family's adjustment to a new part of the country. Could he and they find new friends and make a new life for themselves? All these anxieties combined to sap his energy and reduce his level of productivity in the marketplace.

Other painful feelings resurface at this time. Often job hunters find themselves in situations which provoke their anger. One young woman confessed that she experienced a surge of anger whenever she was interviewed by a person seemingly less experienced and less competent than she was. She was angered by the knowledge that someone with qualifications inferior to hers was making a decision about her employability. This unresolved anger washed over to other interviews where she often overreacted to questions posed by an interviewer, leaving negative impressions and consequently diminishing her effectiveness in the interview.

Unrecognized and unresolved feelings of anger, anxiety, and fear such as the ones indicated in the previous cases can be very destructive and threatening to your emotional well-being. In your job search you will experience many of the same feelings expressed by Don, John, and Jennifer. How best can you deal with them? First, recognize your feelings as you experience them. For those of you unaccustomed to listening to your inner voice, this may be difficult, but the effort to understand will pay dividends in terms of a more satisfying and productive job strategy.

Sometimes you may be too uptight to recognize your feelings. Look for concrete signals like clenched fists, clenched jaws, grinding teeth, temper outbursts, and other behaviors reflecting stress. Monitor your anxiety levels before they become too high and even reduce you to a state of near panic.

Second, allow yourself to experience these feelings rather than practicing denial, which intensifies emotional problems. Studies have been done measuring the effect of a death in the family on the survivors; it was found that the individuals who honestly confronted and worked through their feelings during the grieving process went on to lead more productive and satisfying lives than those who denied their feelings of grief. If, for example, you are anxious about picking up the telephone to make that first call for an informational interview, then admit it. Tell yourself that it's natural to feel uptight, that most of your peers will feel the same way. Anxiety is not a sign of weakness. Then make the call. Watch that anxiety disappear as soon as you succeed at scheduling that coveted interview!

The MBA should take the process of working through his or her feelings a step further through conversations with family and close friends. Venting or talking about feelings has been successful in professional therapy sessions. Given a supportive circle of family and friends, an MBA can use that technique just as successfully as professionals do. Let us suppose that you have just received news that you lost your bid for a job for which you felt preeminently qualified. The news sends you into a rage, with good reason. It's okay for you to go home to your family and say, "I'm really furious. I really thought I was going to get that job . . . management had me in for three interviews . . . practically promised it to me. I know I'm the best qualified and their hiring someone else makes me furious." If you can talk and eliminate your anger in a reasonable length of time, rather than letting it fester, you will be able to dissipate that anger and use your energies and abilities productively. Psychologists warn people not to dwell on negative events. Obsessiveness will cripple an MBA's physical and mental resources and greatly hinder the job campaign.

There are also some other more physical methods for letting off steam. Today many people are involved in physical activities such as running, swimming, aerobic dancing, and weight-lifting. Recognizing the value of their physical and mental well-being, they have built into their day structured periods of relaxation. It is no secret that such periods of relaxation—whether they be in the form of yoga, meditation, or more physical exercise—can dissipate stress before it builds into intolerable proportions.

Often anxieties are accelerated by unrealistic demands and expectations. John's story indicates this aspect. It is easy for an MBA to get carried away by the momentum of the job search and to set unrealistic and demanding goals such as having to send four hundred letters by the end of November, or to see forty potential employers within a six-month period. Arbitrary, unrealistic mandates which, if not met, serve to add to the concerns we already have about accomplishing the goal of finding a job within a certain time. Since psychologists advise us to eliminate all "shoulds" from our vocabulary, this advice can definitely be applied to the job hunt.

One of the most psychologically damaging effects of the job search is the rejection syndrome. Rejections become a way of life. Potential employers deny requests for informational interviews in spite of personal referrals; companies reject requests for an interview; interviewers reject an MBA's candidacy for employment. This barrage of rejections takes its psychological toll, creating a need for an MBA to periodically validate his or her personal worth.

Coping with rejection involves the ability to separate yourself from your profession and your job search. "Your personal worth is *not* being rejected," emphasizes Dr. Christine Merkle, staff psychologist with the Counseling Unit of Boston College's School of Management, who has counseled many MBA students and graduates operating under the stress of job hunting. "People tend to take rejections personally, to feel personally affronted, and blame themselves instead of thinking of the rejection as a mismatch between their skills and the job needs," says Dr. Merkle. "Can every woman with a size nine foot wear a size nine shoe?"

External factors which elude our control also account for the failure to land a job. The mismatch in this case may have to do with personal styles—the chemistry between interviewer and interviewee—rather than professional qualifications. You may be perfectly suited for a job in terms of your qualifications, but if there is a personality clash between you and your potential employer, you can be sure that the job will go to someone else. Luck—being in the right place at the right time—is another factor over which we have no control.

We do not want to give the impression that decisions governing acceptance or rejection are always entirely out of an MBA's control. This is not true. There will be times when an MBA can make changes which alter the impression made in an interview. If this is the case, then the candidate will want to have some feedback about performance during the interview process. We use the following story to illustrate that point. A young woman purchased a smashing suit to wear on a round of interviews for an investment banking job; the skirt had a deep slit in front, as was the fashion of the times. In spite of her excellent qualifications and personality she failed to get a single job offer . . . until a faculty member told her that her skirt was inappropriate for such a traditional industry. She accepted the feedback, purchased a new and more traditional suit, and subsequently received a very good job offer.

In the face of these inner anxieties and outward realities, an MBA's self-esteem demands constant buttressing. To reinforce your self-esteem, periodically reward yourself. In the business world people work for a paycheck, verbal recognition from their supervisor or colleagues, and a sense of accomplishment at the completion of a task. These ingredients are missing during rounds of interviews, until of course a job is obtained. Since the job-hunting process provides no positive reinforcement, other rewards must fill the void. If, for example, you have spent a day composing a very good sales letter, treat yourself to a dinner out. At the end of a difficult day on the telephone tracking down ten people for informational interviews, take yourself to a movie or some other event. Educators have successfully used this system of reward and reinforcement to motivate students in the learning process. Why not apply the same principles to the job-hunting process?

A concrete, hands-on review of your accomplishments on the job hunt will also shore up sagging confidence. You will be amazed at the amount of work you have done when you step back and analyze the extent of your creativity. Bring out all of your letters; total the number of people you have seen and talked with by phone; reflect on the amount of research you have done and the new information you have acquired about companies and industries previously unknown to you; review the successful techniques you have developed to gain access to people; chart your progress in terms of ability to meet new people, handle interviews, and ask and answer pertinent questions. Give yourself credit for all these achievements even though the end of your journey is not yet in sight!

We hope that this chapter has prepared you for the tensions of job hunting, and that you will want to follow our suggestions for dealing with that tension and maximizing your job strategy as a consequence. To do this you must: monitor your feelings of anxiety and cope with them by talking about them; build periods of relaxation into your daily life to prevent tension from building up; lower demands on yourself; and use a system of rewards to recognize your achievement toward your goal of finding the optimal position.

Good luck and good health!

2

Know Thyself: The Need for Self-Assessment

Starting a job search is frightening for almost every MBA. For many, it is the first major plunge into the job market. At best, it is an unfamiliar process, and it is a good idea for you to rethink the entire MBA program and consider why you got involved in it originally. You will be surprised at how much you have learned. This should not only give you more confidence, but it will help you obtain the correct position.

While the MBA degree certainly does not ensure an optimal position, it does provide the technique, know-how, and confidence that will help you obtain one. (A woman or minority MBA will particularly find that the degree means even greater entry to an ever-expanding market.) While many employers are becoming less and less impressed with an MBA degree *per se*, they are still very much impressed with the people who hold that degree. An MBA has matured, has learned to ask endless questions in a probing way, and has developed perspectives on his or her own strengths and weaknesses. Some MBAs have acquired valuable management experience via in-

---

ternships, jobs, and summer employment. Every MBA probably should have gained specific functional tools in areas such as accounting and control, computer science, marketing research, financial analysis, and investments. Even more importantly, an MBA has been trained to think, to analyze, and to make decisions.

An MBA is hired for both present and future capabilities. While the degree is no longer a guarantee of a position, membership in the "MBA Club" does indicate greater capabilities and ability to think conceptually. In addition to the subjective qualities enhanced and mentioned above, an MBA has learned to digest large volumes of complicated material, to become a problem-solver, and to make strategic decisions. An MBA also has learned to work with people on major projects involving complicated cases and sometimes real company problems; this work develops teamwork and cooperation. An MBA has learned how to inspire peers, build them up when necessary, and get tough with nonproductive members. The MBA has worked in school groups such as graduate management associations and for authority figures such as members of faculty and administration.

In all these activities the MBA has learned how to communicate. Most programs are heavily saturated with discussion, with listening to peers as well as to faculty. Expressing ideas becomes second nature to an MBA. Good diction, spelling, and grammar are apparent and are indeed mandatory.

Working without close supervision is par for the course. This is one reason why some MBAs develop authority problems on the job. An MBA is a self-starter who is motivated, persistent, and tenacious with an ability to follow through. An MBA knows how to manage time and accomplish the task with minimal questions.

How many people have been able to develop the perspective you have from your MBA degree? You know what it is to intensively read newspapers, business periodicals, magazines, studies, and books. As a member of an elite group you have been exposed to broad perspectives including those of a social nature. In short you have a wide range of interests and have even developed community concerns.

Not only have you matured but you are much more aware of yourself. You have goals even if they are constantly being revised. You have balance and are not easily swept off your feet. You have tasted setbacks; you know what it is to lose and yet rebound. You are realistic, having spent a fairly long period of time dealing in realities; there is very little room in an MBA program for vague theory without being challenged by both peers and faculty. You know how to accept responsibility, and you know how to delegate. Your judgment is far sounder and sharper than before you entered the program. You know the importance of being courteous and how to use this quality in a positive business way. You have heard many speakers from business; you have met several executives-in-residence. These people represent a job network for you.

Creativity

There are two areas that are important for the MBA to remember and constantly put into practice. The first is to be creative. When MBAs are creative, they are being different in positive and innovative ways. Generally an MBA can control the destiny of a job, instead of the job controlling the MBA.

What does being creative mean? It requires using talents you haven't been in the habit of using. It is going beyond customary job definitions. Creativity is pulling together all your diverse talents and attributes, and implementing a job campaign which will be different from any MBA competitor's. Creativity in your job campaign means pulling together your values, skills and traits, and accomplishments in a manner which will prompt prospective employers to notice you quickly. Creative MBAs seek new ways to implement a campaign. Of course they are never afraid of trying new things, of embarking on a new trail if they think it will be better.

Creative young executives don't hesitate at all to expand the horizons of a new job. These MBA executives, while remaining realistic, always throw out new ideas as a way of setting themselves apart and making money for their companies. Creativity is the ability to focus on new ideas.

Being creative means not being tied to exact systems. It is thinking freely and imaginatively. Fresh and original ideas followed by careful execution are the best career path to follow. An MBA should not worry about being nonscientific during a job campaign, nor should an MBA be hung up with titles and job descriptions. No two people perform the same job in the same way.

Picture your career with symbols rather than terminology. Reflect on what you're looking for, when, and with whom. Think in concepts. Consider all the things you do and are interested in. These may give you clues to the job which will be best for you.

Think broadly in several different areas rather than becoming confined to one. And don't be too critical, at least not initially, when you brainstorm new thoughts.

Dream once in a while—dream even the impossible dream. Industry is filled with unimaginative people who do things by the numbers. But you can be sure that every top executive has known how to deviate once in awhile.

Is there a formula for being creative? Not really. Look for new ways to use an existing approach. Perhaps this can be in interview preparation: you do the interviewing. Can you change an existing approach to something such as your résumé? Can you expand on an existing approach? Can you substitute one thing for another? Can you use the telephone cleverly instead of a cover letter?

Don't hesitate to challenge apparent axioms. Never forget to break a problem down into smaller parts in order to be creative in one of those parts.

Taking Risks

Taking risks is the second important aspect to remember and put into practice. The executive who succeeds is one who lives with bearable stress and takes intelligent risks. It is fallacious to think that intelligent people avoid risks; a successful career is impossible without calculated risks.

Risk-taking has some very important implications. It means that the MBA executive has an open mind, is receptive to opportunities and personal changes, and is able to optimize every ability. Of course an MBA does everything possible to eliminate potential problems. But if risks are not taken, the best starting position will not be obtained, and there will be no growth in this position.

Leaders do not avoid risks; rather, they seek intelligent ones. Therefore, one thing you should project in your résumé and in your interviews is that you are a wise risk-taker.

There are several kinds of risk-takers: those who are very careful, conservative, and opt for minimum chance of failure; and those who are ready to shoot dice almost any time, sometimes too quickly. There are those who are careful risk-takers, and there are those who will take an occasional risk prudently. Your nature will dictate the most comfortable category for you. Once you have determined this, you should train yourself to be "prudently adventurous"!

You won't enjoy the excitement of a top job without taking some risks. It may mean moving to another city or to an industry or company not previously considered. If you take a job that looks especially familiar before you go to work, you may be safe but you will probably become bored very quickly.

And remember that your job selection is the first of many risks. If you do not want to take any risks, you should reconsider your choice of business as a career.

General Procedure

The skills, knowledge, personal talents, and attributes you possess are indeed all a part of you, but perhaps, like most MBAs, you have not had a chance to take stock in an organized way. Perhaps you ask, "Where will the classroom and extracurricular experiences lead?" To help you answer this question and to continue the planning stage of the career launch, we feel a rigorous self-assessment is very important. It may take time, yes, but in the end you will have accomplished one more step in the process. Your "self" will become better defined. You will understand better where your schooling has led. Finally, your positive self-image will be reconstructed after several years of rigorous studies or work experience.

How should you start?

First, write an autobiography. It should be complete and should emphasize hobbies and extracurricular activities—everything you have enjoyed. Highlight your achievements. This will not only make you feel good about yourself, but will give you an important indication of what you want to do. You will use this list continuously in writing your résumé and in controlling job interviews.

Be sure to examine your feelings about the present: what is good for you, what is not so good. What do you really like doing? Peruse many of the occupational directions in the business library. These can indicate career possibilities.

Make an elaborate listing of what you would like to have happen to you in the future. Spend some time listing all the things that you wish to accomplish in your lifetime. Then analyze a recent accomplishment that has brought great enjoyment.

Make sure you are dealing with job *concept* and *content*, not with job titles. Understand that a career is primarily based on skills and that a job is simply problems to be solved. Skills and interest will dictate the career options which need to be prioritized. While you can come up with more than one option, in the job search you will want to work at only one option at a time.

Specific Self-Assessment

Take a good, long look at what you have jotted down and what you have thought along the way. Usually, after having gone through the preceding steps, an MBA has a feeling of understanding and self-confidence. While the previous exercise is relatively brief, it yields a large amount of vital information. More structured activities aimed specifically at the MBA career are found in the self-assessment exercises on pages 13–17. These exercises act as a bridge between the preliminary assessment suggestions noted earlier and the later steps of résumé and cover-letter writing discussed in Chapters 5 and 6. Work with these two exercises carefully, slowly, and honestly and be prepared for a very positive outcome.

You can probably see certain trends from having completed the self-assessment exercises. One thing is for certain: if you were unclear about your understanding of yourself, these exercises will have given clarity and will probably indicate areas in which you have been successful. Even though some of the revelations may have been painful, it is only by thoroughly understanding oneself that the MBA can successfully approach the job market.

With this clearer, organized view of yourself, the next step, discussed in Chapter 3, is to formulate some solid career objectives. These will enable you to search for your optimal job, but also will help you avoid an increasingly common problem facing some MBAs, especially on their first job: disenchantment and a feeling of no challenge after about a year. Armed with the tools already discussed and the ones yet to come, you'll find your job will be a great one.

SELF-ASSESSMENT EXERCISE 1*

Answer the following questions honestly and carefully; write down insights on a separate piece of paper. These will help guide you in constructing your résumé and cover letter.

1. What have been your most satisfying and most disappointing graduate school (MBA) experiences? Most satisfying and disappointing work experiences?

2. Do you like to work with figures and other details?

3. What type of temperament do you possess?

4. In which past accomplishments do you take pride?

---

* *These exercises were a part of a paper entitled "A Job Campaign Guide For Boston College MBA's—A Self-Marketing Model," prepared for a class in Market Analysis and Models by Joseph A. O'Brien.*

5. Can you express yourself clearly in conversation?

6. Do you enjoy making presentations to groups?

7. What motivates you? fear? money? praise? Other?

8. Are your abilities more creative or mechanical?

9. Do you prefer individual or group projects?

10. Do you prefer to work with people or data?

11. How have you changed since beginning graduate school?

12. Are you easily offended or hurt?

13. Is it easier for you to express your thoughts verbally or in writing?

14. How have you demonstrated leadership potential?

15. How important to you is prestige and status?

16. Why did you decide to pursue an MBA degree?

17. Why did you select a particular concentration?

18. What abilities of yours do people most often praise?

19. What habits of yours do people most often criticize?

20. How do you spend your leisure time?

21. Do you prefer independence or association?

22. How confident are you in your abilities?

SELF-ASSESSMENT EXERCISE 2

Using your responses from Exercise 1 as a guideline, you should now proceed to develop a *personal inventory*. A personal inventory is a private, introspective, written self-analysis you can employ to realistically assess your career potential.

1. Prepare an extensive chronological narrative. Explain why you made certain career decisions in the past; i.e., choice of your MBA degree program, concentration.

2. Make a statement of your personal values.

3. Summarize your personal philosophy.

4. Prepare a brief outline of your career plans for the next five years.

5. Write a broad statement about your life goals.

After completing Exercise 2, the following questions should be answered:

1. Where have you lived geographically?

2. What is your estimate of the quality of living in these areas?

3. Has there been a noticeable trend to where you have lived?

4. What has been your own family background? How has this background affected your own attitudes, values, and life-style?

5. What is the status of your health? Has poor health ever gotten in the way of your accomplishing your goals?

6. What kinds of schools have you attended? What have been their effects on your attitudes and skills?

7. As you review your personal growth, have your decisions reflected soundness and maturity?

8. What types of people have influenced your decisions?

9. Are there gaps in your education and experience? If yes, why? And for how long? Do you consider these gaps significant either negatively or positively?

10. What interests and challenges you?

11. What do you do best and what do you like to do?

12. Are you a leader? What leadership roles have you had?

13. What traits do you admire in people?

14. How do you feel about people in positions of authority?

15. If you are a man, would you work for a woman or, if you are a woman, would you work for a man?

16. Do you consider your energy level high?

17. Do you think your career goals (if you have them) are attainable?

18. How well do you use your skills?

19. Are you an over-achiever?

20. What kinds of jobs have you held part- or full-time?

21. What did you learn at your jobs?

22. Did you distinguish yourself at work? How?

23. Why did you leave your jobs?

24. Do you have direction to your life?

25. Do you give up easily?

26. Can you handle criticism?

27. Do you avoid responsibilities?

28. Describe the qualities of the best supervisor you have ever had. Describe the worst.

29. Describe the qualities of the best professor you have ever had. Describe the worst.

30. What is your leadership style?

31. How do you get along with peers? Why?

32. What kind of environment do you need to be effective?

33. What kinds of people do you like to work with?

34. What is important to you?

35. How do you spend your time?

36. If you have had one really good job experience, why was it better than others?

37. What things are important to you in your relations with others?

38. Were your mother and father leaders? How did they affect your values? How did they use authority?

39. How important is money to you?

40. Do you have financial objectives for the next five years?

41. What influences have your parents had on your values, beliefs, and career plans?

3

What Do You Want to Do?

By this time you should have some idea of how to address the number one question, "What do you want to do?" You must decide the answer yourself after going through self-assessment processes such as the ones in Chapter 2. Not having a specific career goal can cause you to make an impression of indecisiveness. Vague objectives on a résumé or in interviews can create doubt in a prospective employer's mind. Not determining your goals in life, not having an understanding of yourself, not thinking about your long-range objectives, or not taking control of your life will make it impossible for you to determine what your objectives are and what you want to do.

Don't just talk strategy—write it down! Be as specific as possible, yet don't worry that some things are not exact. When your thoughts are written down, your family, friends, or faculty person can help shape them. Also, a written strategy implies commitment. Such a plan requires knowing yourself. It means having an appreciation of the business environment and knowing what positions and career tracks are available. It means understanding what you are able to handle. Finally, it involves recognizing what you want to do and having the courage to go after it. The only real responsibility you have is to yourself—to fulfill your hopes and aspirations and those of your family.

The Role of Learning

One of the most important things to remember as you plan your career is that you are just starting to learn. This may seem strange after finishing six years of classroom work, but it is true nonetheless. You are embarking on some terribly important decisions with relatively little background in the area. Therefore, you must be willing to learn from a variety of sources: books such as this one, peers, faculty, informational interviews,* friends, and family. Not everyone finds learning easy. By getting into the process early you will start trying and experimenting. By observing your peers and by reading about the entire area as you are now doing, you will feel increasingly comfortable. By reading trade periodicals, magazines, and newspapers, you will learn about industries and companies. All of this is part of the learning process.

As was previously mentioned, having enough time to formulate and carry out your job strategy is of paramount importance. It takes most MBAs nine to twelve months to learn these new skills and to execute a game plan. Being able to space the process over a long time is a real benefit. Also remember that this entire task is new to everyone at one time or another, and many new things are fairly complex.

Listen carefully to what is being said—whether by a faculty advisor or company official. Listening is difficult for most of us some of the time, but it becomes particularly hard when you are embroiled in the intensity of a job search. It may seem elementary to mention, but be certain that you are capturing the flavor of important conversations, digesting the speaker's main points and noting why they are being made, plus determining whether or not the points are supportable. It is often helpful to restate the important elements to make sure they are clearly understood.

Factors That Affect Your Career Strategy

EXTERNAL INFLUENCES

There are, of course, many external factors that influence an MBA's career strategy. Changing environments will influence career opportu-

---

* *An informational interview is one you initiate with an executive in order to gain knowledge about a field or a type of job. It is distinct from the job interview whose primary objective is the selection of new personnel. More about these interviews on page 39.*

nities, and constantly improving technology has implications for career strategy as well. For example, improved medical technology may
mean longer life and possibly second, third, and even fourth career
implications.

The changing economic situation has perhaps the most dramatic implications. What types of skills and people will be in demand?
What areas of the economy will be most active? In business education
the emphasis has shifted some from marketing to finance and computers because of inflation and cost stress. A few years ago there was
an oil shortage, today, at least for the moment, there is an oil glut. In
developing your career strategy, be aware of these kinds of changes.

The political scene influences business and career strategies
greatly, even in days of reduced government involvement. Defense
spending affects some businesses. Legislation applies to certain industries more than others. Recent legislation makes owning your own
business more attractive than it used to be. New pension legislation
can inspire career mobility between companies at later ages.

Shifting cultural trends also influence job strategies. The
new phenomenon of the dual-career couple has opened up significant
executive opportunities both for women and for businesses. And it is
no longer unusual to see people achieving honors and rewards in
several diverse careers.

PERSONAL MOTIVATIONS

What you want to do and the field in which you are motivated to
excel are the most important factors in developing your career strategy, but of course not to the exclusion of other things.

Most MBAs are not theoretical. They are business people
interested in accomplishment and profit. A few have a great interest
in the arts or in people for people's sake, and for this small group
there exists small but increasing opportunity in the nonprofit sector.
Of course many business persons have strong extracurricular interest
in the nonprofit sector.

Donald Super's terminology* uses terms describing a wide
variety of business positions. See how you relate to each of these terms.

> *Achievement:* A value associated with "work which gives one
> a feeling of accomplishment in doing a job well."

> *Altruism:* A value or goal that is present in "work which en-
> ables one to contribute to the welfare of others."

* Work Values Inventory Roster, *Boston: Houghton Mifflin, 1970, pp. 8–10.*

Associates: A value characterized by "work which brings one into contact with fellow workers whom he likes."

Creativity: A value associated with "work which permits one to invent new things, design new products, or develop new ideas."

Economic return: A value or goal associated with "work which pays well and enables one to have the things he wants."

Esthetics: A value inherent in "work which permits one to make beautiful things and to contribute beauty to the world."

Independence: Associated with "work which permits one to work in his own way, as fast or as slowly as he wishes."

Intellectual stimulation: Associated with "work which provides opportunity for independent thinking and for learning how and why things work."

Management: Associated with "work which permits one to plan and lay out work for others to do."

Prestige: Associated with "work which gives one standing in the eyes of others and evokes respect."

Security: Associated with "work which provides one with the certainty of having a job even in hard times."

Supervisory relations: A value associated with "work which is carried out under a supervisor who is fair and with whom one can get along."

Surroundings: A value associated with "work which is carried out under pleasant conditions—not too hot or too cold, noisy, dirty, etc."

Variety: Associated with "work that provides an opportunity to do different types of jobs."

Way of life: Associated with the kind of work that "permits one to live the kind of life he or she chooses and to be the type of person he or she wishes to be."

Once an MBA recognizes that a good strategy means positive and intense commitment, it soon becomes obvious that the best of all combinations is matching desire with what is in demand. An MBA's only obligation to society (or anyone for that matter) is to select a professional area which personally interests, excites, and motivates and which relates to the needs of the business environment. Of course this joy of doing what you want to do and being successful at it may also bring the desire to work outside your professional area on a volunteer basis to help improve the lives of others. This outside effort will complement your business role and might even enhance it.

Resources

When assessing career options, start with an open mind and do not overlook any area of interest. The *Occupational Outlook Handbook*, published by the U.S. Department of Labor, presents some career ideas for your initial consideration. In addition, major newspapers in key American cities present career opportunities in the classified help-wanted columns and in the financial sections. Your university placement office, faculty, and family can give you ideas. Trade magazines and periodicals are additional sources of information. Once you've found a potential area of interest, obtain appropriate books, trade magazines, or newspaper articles so that you can become more familiar with it.

There is also a great deal of information about career tracks in other readily available materials: annual reports, company house organs, trade magazines, newspapers, and biographical sketches of successful company executives, for example. Obtain all the material available so that you can expand your career knowledge.

Your business school library and other libraries in the city should have these materials. The libraries also have references related to job hunting including industry books, employment directories, annual reports, and a variety of catalogues. Remember to use the reference librarian as well as *Subject Collections: A Guide to Special Book Collections in Libraries*. The library research will give you a perspective on the past and a feeling for the future.

An MBA can also research a particular career area by checking with professional organizations through the directories they publish. In addition, many areas in management have societies and national groups, such as the American Management Association and the American Marketing Association. Other resources are books that describe many occupational areas in detail. Also, complete reference books for periodicals such as the *Reader's Guide to Periodical Literature, The New York Times Index* and the *Wall Street Journal Index* are published. These indexes allow you to research magazine and newspaper articles pertinent to your career choice. There are professional groups you can join which will put you in contact with many people who have valuable information. Current periodicals such as the *Wall Street Journal, U.S. News and World Report, Business Week, Fortune,* and *The New York Times* provide information on occupations that are expanding and those that are waning. Through careful research, you can even acquire information on potential executives for whom you may work.

Another way to accumulate information on career paths and occupations is through observation. Observe while in school, by visiting companies and institutions, through internships, through part-time work, through academically sponsored major projects, through volunteer work, and by being in contact with potential employers. An MBA can be a successful observer by cultivating a sense of curiosity. Offer few opinions and *listen.* The more intimately acquainted you are with career data, the more intelligently you can ask and answer questions in the later all-important job interview.

The Future: A Range of Choices

A variety of major careers in business are available with varying growth potential. It is important for you to choose one that to you is rewarding and interesting, one that will make you excited about going to work every day. A good career choice is one in which you really enjoy spending the sixty to seventy hours per week initially working to facilitate a fast career track. Since the choice of career is often directly related to the choice of major in the MBA program, the career options are discussed in this section along basic functional lines in business: accounting, computer science, finance, marketing, human-resource management, production and purchasing, and other special careers.

ACCOUNTING CAREERS

One career field often overlooked by MBAs is accounting. Since the profitability of any business is dependent on the flow of money through the firm, and more specifically how this money is used, accounting is an extremely important area in all businesses regardless of their size. From a small company making awnings for commercial buildings to a multinational corporation selling diverse product lines in twenty-eight countries, or from a small town government with 3,000 inhabitants to the large federal government of the United States, every entity needs to know where the money is being used. The depth and the breadth of the career field can probably best be understood when you consider that over 900,000 individuals presently work in management accounting, with about 10 to 15 percent of these certified internal auditors.

An MBA can consider three types of accounting careers: a corporate career, a government career, or a public accounting career. While each of these has some similarities, they are indeed distinctive enough that the MBA should carefully define his or her ultimate career objective before deciding which to enter. Individuals in corporate accounting careers are in-house people who take care of the company's financial records providing the finanical information others in the firm need for sound business decisions. These MBAs are sometimes called corporate, industrial, management, or private accountants. Important areas of specialization in this field include budgeting, internal auditing, investments, and taxation. Probably one of the most rapidly expanding areas involves the design, implementation, and operation of a computerized business accounting system.

Government accounting careers can be in either the federal, state, or local government. Accounting in this field consists of examining the operations of the many government agencies or the auditing of individuals and businesses who do business with the federal government and of those who are subject to government regulation. Owing to the immense amount of red tape, the entering pay levels, civil service requirements, and the limited opportunity for fast-track advancement, fewer MBAs enter this career field.

The final career path in accounting—public accounting—is the one most frequently entered by MBAs. Public accountants work for independent accounting firms, some of which are owned by individuals while others have as many as 650 partners. Public accountants usually specialize in auditing, tax matters, or accounting systems. After a period of time an MBA sometimes leaves the public accounting firm to work full time for the client whom he or she was advising.

It appears that the overall demand for accountants, particularly those with computer science and systems expertise, will grow at a very rapid rate throughout the 1980s. As managers rely more and more on accounting information to make sound business decisions, and as it becomes more and more difficult to make a profit, MBA accountants will be in increasing demand.

COMPUTER SCIENCE CAREERS

Every corporation, governmental unit, and nonprofit organization is becoming more dependent on efficient methods of processing and storing data. The need in this field is indicated by the more than 180,000 systems analysts and 250,000 programmers now working, and by new job opportunities expanding at a rate of about 5 to 7 percent per year. While of course most of these are not MBAs, as an MBA you have a choice of two broad career areas: systems analysis and programming.

Both MBA programmers and systems analysts specialize in computer business applications. These applications range from creating the programs and systems needed to run the company's payroll or accounts receivable to programs for operating and controlling the company's inventory and production scheduling. As is apparent, the MBA pursuing a career in this field should be as knowledgeable as possible in the various functional areas (accounting, finance, marketing, and production).

More specifically, systems analysts design, implement, and oversee the use of a new system of computer programming. Basically these MBAs analyze and solve the problem at hand using such techniques as cost accounting, linear programming, and sampling. The design of a new system often proceeds as follows: design the system in an outline form; prepare charts and diagrams describing the operations of the systems as well as its costs and benefits; translate the system's requirements into the capabilities of computer machinery available or needed; and prepare overall program specifications and procedures. Because the problems are so varied and complex, a systems analyst must have technical knowledge, logical thinking ability, and a background in mathematics.

Programming is an area that few MBAs enter mainly because the job usually does not require an MBA degree. This is of course reflected in lower starting salaries and slower advancement. However, this field does provide an opportunity for an MBA to gain an entry position that can lead to other positions in the company or in the computer industry in general. Programmers are responsible for writing the detailed step-by-step procedures and programs needed once the overall system has been developed. Programmers, as well as systems analysts, can advance to management-level positions in the data processing department or in any of the other functional business areas of the company. In addition, broadly skilled and adaptable programmers and systems analysts probably have one of the best opportunities for career switching because demand right now and probably for the next five years promises to be extremely high for computer-trained and -oriented executives.

FINANCE CAREERS

One career area actively pursued by many MBAs is finance. Careers in this field are in banking, corporate finance, or securities analysis. MBAs in banking make business decisions within existing federal and state laws and regulations. In addition to supervising financial activities, bank managers usually participate in a wide variety of community projects. The choice of banking careers is commensurate with the many services offered; these include loan officers (who evaluate credit and collateral of individuals and businesses to determine whether or not a loan should be made), operations officers (who study ways to improve the bank's productivity thereby upgrading the bank's performance), and trust officers (who do investment research, invest funds, and advise individuals and companies).

There are more than 300,000 bank officers in the United States with a 5 to 10 percent annual increase in positions expected throughout the 1980s. There are indeed excellent opportunities in banking, with MBAs having the inside track for moving ahead rapidly.

Careers in corporate finance are often quite similar to those in corporate accounting. An MBA in corporate finance analyzes the financial condition of the company and makes recommendations on needed cost reductions. In addition he or she determines the most effective way for the company to obtain the short- or long-term capital needed. A corporate finance position generally gives the MBA excellent company exposure, and it is a way of moving into upper-level management positions in finance (such as to comptroller or vice-president of finance) as well as into other functional areas.

A career in finance as a securities analyst involves working for a bank, investment house, or private corporation. Generally an MBA degree is required for an entry-level position. Security analysts study securities and develop buy, sell, or hold recommendations for them. This information is then passed on to a security broker—a salesperson dealing in stocks, bonds, and other instruments of value, who earns a commission on the transaction. There are some excellent opportunities for advancement in this field, particularly when working for a bank or a private corporation.

Most senior business executives feel a strong affinity for financial areas because today's company, regardless of its makeup, is strongly involved in money matters. Whether the problem affecting the firm is financing inventory and receivables, effecting a merger, or moving into the market place with a new product, financing is involved.

Opportunities in the various financial areas are extensive. In banking, in addition to the positions mentioned, work in financial analysis is important and rewarding. Handling the bank's securities, loans for commercial real estate, and bank data processing offers great opportunity.

The area of investments also provides career opportunities for MBAs. Corporate bonds, municipal bonds, mutual funds, government securities, and commodity futures are all areas which have good career possibilities.

HUMAN RESOURCES MANAGEMENT CAREERS

The human resources management field is a good one for MBAs interested in personnel, industrial relations, or labor relations. This career involves establishing personnel policies, setting up and administrating salary and other benefits, hiring and training personnel, negotiating with labor unions, and developing and interpreting labor law.

MARKETING CAREERS

The broad area of marketing probably employs the most MBA graduates. Sales, all too frequently ignored, is one good career area that also pays very well. Recruiting, hiring, training, sales supervision, developing compensatory plans, sales forecasting, budgeting, and sales promotion are all sales management responsibilities. Many sales managers become marketing vice-presidents.

Making forecasts, conducting market research, and developing marketing plans are other good areas for such careers. Product management and product line development are important areas to any company. Also, direct mail and in-the-home merchandising opportunities are expanding at a rapid rate. The retail industry offers very rapid advancement and high compensation. The communications (advertising) area of marketing is a career field unto itself. Advertising agencies, agency work, industrial advertising, corporate and product advertising, radio and television advertising (particularly cable TV), sales promotion, and publicity campaigns are excellent career areas.

Many MBA graduates with undergraduate degrees in engineering find themselves in project engineering and new process development, or as liaison executives in new product development. They are involved in product and package design as well as in design consultation. Also, an engineering background combined with MBA training is excellent background for a career as a sales engineer in the industrial products field.

PRODUCTION AND PURCHASING CAREERS

Plant management, production management, inventory management, production and material control, and purchasing are all good, demanding areas requiring skilled MBAs who usually have strong quantitative backgrounds and capabilities.

SPECIAL CAREERS

Numerous special career paths are available to an MBA; consulting is an expanding and exciting one. Strategic planning, corporate development, and appraisal are frequently jobs taken on by consulting companies. Labor, market, and expense forecasting are also important consulting assignments. As mentioned in the accounting area, a number of large, prestigious public accounting firms are setting up separate consulting divisions specializing in operations analysis and research and systems and procedures work where MBAs are used almost exclusively. Many consulting firms are beginning to do extensive work in transportation analysis, distribution cost analysis, physical distribution analysis, manufacturing analysis, and systems technology.

With consumer credit at an all-time high, sophisticated credit management, accounts receivable financing, and credit promotion are all growing MBA areas. Industrial engineering and production management employ many MBAs. Production control, systems design and development, and R and D application to total product planning also employ some MBAs. Appropriation engineering and engineering forecasts and budgets attract a few others.

The health-care field, with today's rising costs, is one where there is a strong need for modern business management. Administrative work, medical liaison work, budgeting, accounting, finance, and personnel administration all are attractive MBA career paths in this field.

The insurance industry also has opportunities for MBAs. Life, group, pension, home medical, general, marine, fire and theft all are part of a growth industry.

For those with combined MBA and JD degrees, corporate law, patent law, banking law, real estate law, anti-trust and contract law, labor relations law, and security law all have opportunities available. The job can be in a corporate setting, with a labor union, in a private law firm, or for government. There is a growing need for people with the combined-degree background.

In the nonprofit sector, business managers for music groups, theater art groups, ballet companies, and museums are always on the lookout for the MBAs oriented to this type of work.

Real estate has shown more monetary growth in the last twenty years in the United States than any other product or service. Acquisitions, negotiations, market analysis, financing, options, mortgages, leases, property administration, sales, brokerage, appraisal—all these represent opportunity. In addition, there are real possibilities in this area for owning your own business.

As increasing numbers of MBAs also have MSW degrees, social agencies—particularly today with reduced government aid—need business-trained executives with social service interests to manage them. As is indicated in this section, the problem for the MBA is not having a choice; it is really in deciding what you want.

How Demands and Expectations Relate to Your Strategy

Start relating the demands and the expectations of certain careers to yourself. For example, some sales managers are away from home a great deal. If you are a homebody, this career isn't for you. But if you decide to be a sales manager, understand you will have to make certain adjustments and sacrifices. You must determine the changes you'll have to make, and then decide if they are worth the price. It's amazing, for example, to hear young executives in the retail industry complaining about the long hours. How could they even contemplate this industry, assuming they had done some background career work, and not understand that it is a service catering to consumers on a six- or seven-day basis?

Once you have gone through all this highly personal preparation, do some dreaming. Put down in order of importance what you do best; what you are comfortable doing; what you want to do. Then pretend you can have anything you want. What would you select? If this does not seem at all plausible, select the next one and so on until you have delineated a reliable goal. Having determined the goals you want and which ones look realistic or for which you are willing to make concessions, establish an objective.

Reflection

There are some questions you should ask as you review your long-term career plans. Am I stressing areas that can mean success as I define it? What are the failure possibilities? What outside help do I need? Have I done everything possible to familiarize myself with the industries in which I am interested?

Even though career strategy is a highly personal affair, frank peer-group discussion can be very helpful. Don't ignore this type of outside resource. Peer groups can be very helpful when you are constantly checking whether you are going in the right direction. However, remember that in the last analysis the career is yours. It is very personal; it reflects your style, your needs, and your desires.

4

Getting on Track

You can see that the career-strategy operation is one of researching pertinent information, evaluating the factors involved, and accomplishing all of this on a predetermined schedule. Once you've chosen your career and set your ultimate goals, you must determine the path you wish to follow.

Paths to the Top

Looking for the greatest training program or the fastest track is not always the best start. It is preferable that you select an area of a business which interests you, which has potential leading to top management, and for which you qualify. Examine the particular jobs along the career route and trace all possible paths. For example, in a retail department store, an MBA merchandising career path might look like the following:

Chairman of the Board and Chief Executive Officer
↑
President
↑
Vice-President and General Merchandise Manager
↑

Divisional Merchandise Manager

↑

Store Manager

↑

Divisional Merchandise Manager for one store

↑

Buyer

↑

Department Manager for one store

↑

Senior Assistant Manager

In the same department store, a career path in labor relations and human resources management might be:

Vice-President Human Resources Management

↑

Director of Liaison Relations

↑

Director of Personnel

↑

Assistant Director of Personnel

↑

Director of Executive Recruiting

↑

Director of Fringe Benefits

↑

Director of Compensation

↑

Employment Manager

↑

Wage and Salary Administrator

↑

Director of Employee Relations

↑

Staff Assistant to Personnel Director

An MBA career in marketing in a consumer goods company could take the following path:

Vice-President for Marketing and Sales
↑
Director of Market Research
↑
Product Manager
↑
Assistant Product Manager
↑
Sales Manager
↑
Sales Representative
↑
Market Analyst

Other possible career tracks in an advertising agency, commercial banking, and investment banking are indicated below:

ADVERTISING AGENCY

Vice-President for Specific Accounts
↑
Account Executive
↑
Assistant Account Executive
↑
Media Buyer
↑
Production Assistant
↑
Advertising Research
↑
Sales for Consumer Goods Package Company

COMMERCIAL BANKING

> Vice-President
>
> ↑
>
> Commercial Loan Officer
>
> ↑
>
> Retail Loan Officer
>
> ↑
>
> Investment Assistant
>
> ↑
>
> Credit Marketing Assistant
>
> ↑
>
> General Study of Banking Business

INVESTMENT BANKING

> Vice-President
>
> ↑
>
> Securities Negotiator
>
> ↑
>
> Bond Analyst
>
> ↑
>
> Sales Broker

Determine the length of time for such upward mobility and also the time lateral moves will take. However, the time it takes to get to the top should not be your only determination. What you do along the track is equally, if not more, important. Some careers have slower job tracks but they may generate greater job satisfaction.

Don't concentrate too much on the short-run prestige of a job and company and thus neglect your long-term career path. While an MBA need not always follow the long-term route, it should at least be carefully considered. Know your options.

Plan Your Career Moves

Simply learning the specifics of certain career tracks, while very important, is not enough. Planning your way to the top involves much more. A career planner is a wise MBA and executive, not a ruthless opportunist, and this type of thinking is as important to you as strategic planning would be to your company. If you have charted a course, you will have choices when the time comes for decisions.

Career planning is more art than science. It involves plotting goals and setting interim objectives. This means keeping track of your progress and making revisions when necessary. The planning stage can cover any period of your career, but the most likely is the first six years. It can include hopes for additional education and intentions for doing community work. It should also include your salary objectives. And, most important, you should really have *more* than one plan so that you can see all your options. Why all this thought? Because you should never abdicate the responsibility of planning your own career.

What are some of the things you look for when selecting a career track, an industry, a company, an occupation? For each possibility, ask yourself the following questions:

1. Are you going to supervise any people? What kinds of people? How many?

2. What salary are you likely to start with? What kind of salary progress will take place? Salary information is available from the placement office, peers, recruiters, and the school's alumni.

3. What job title will you have at the beginning and then later on? There is nothing wrong with being title conscious but don't become obsessed with it.

When considering a job, have both the job description and its specifications. The *description* delineates the duties and responsibilities of the job; the *specifications* list the qualifications for it, including education, previous experience, language requirements, and specific MBA concentration. It also often gives the salary range.

The earlier you start this process, the better—best before you leave your MBA program. Pick your industry carefully. Think about its growth potential and find out how it fits into your compensation picture. For example, the top jobs in industries such as utilities and meat processing pay well under the average. However, don't worry as much about money as about the company's management and reputation. Unless you are going to have an exceptionally prestigious job, stay away from a troubled company.

A big company is probably a better entry spot than a small

one. If you resist becoming too specialized, you'll be exposed to more professional management practices. Moreover, big-name company experience will probably enhance your résumé.

Aim for a position in which the total business can be viewed as quickly as possible. Some people feel business is learned from the top down. Good jobs for this overview are assistant to the president, a corporate staff position at the start, investment banking, or consulting.

Make sure you fit in the job and that you are visible. Avoid situations involving total immersion in the administration of trivia. Instead seek out situations which permit you to broaden your horizons.

Find a spot where you can operate as part of a team. Executives usually move up in two's and three's, bringing with them their key subordinates, who are considered crucial to their effectiveness and mobility.

Seek an environment which tells you how you are doing. Only from intelligent and constructive feedback can you grow. Also, have a close association with your supervisors. This allows you to work in the context of a larger segment of the business.

Know what your job is and what you are responsible for. Be accountable for your work. Only then can you measure your own growth and, of course, be measured by your supervisor.

Be a decision maker and be in a decision-making role no matter how small the decisions. Develop special expertise.

Plan to leave your specialty within, say, three years, unless you want to remain specialized for your entire career. Remember that your MBA degree trained you to be a general manager. Be a specialist at the beginning and get some technical credentials. But as soon as you can, get into a generalist situation.

Early in your career, plan to move through several functions—production, sales, and research and development. Also, get financial experience as early as possible. Top managers work with and deal in numbers.

As mentioned previously, your plan should include additional education. You can do this in two ways. First, keep abreast of all current business, political, and social news. Second, never consider the MBA a terminal degree. Take courses periodically in various areas of business. New techniques, particularly quantitative ones, are continuously being introduced. You might even try a political science course or an art or music class.

Protect yourself from getting set too geographically or becoming company-immobile. Most MBAs change jobs at least once in the first five years after graduation. While you'll probably have more company loyalty as you move up the ladder, remember that most presidents come from outside their new company.

As you develop your plan, write it down. This can help focus you on fundamental goals, a crucial element in your career charting. Fill in all the details. A charted career plan should incorporate your goals, achievements, and aspirations. Only after you have depicted these can you establish a timetable.

Mentor Relationship

Line experience in companies is usually the shortest route to the top. Training programs are fine if they are outstanding (however most are not). But one of the best tracks is a line position with training seminars and a boss who is supportive, who teaches you, and who wants you to grow.

Some MBAs may have been farsighted enough to have developed a mentor relationship during their undergraduate days, while in the MBA program, or while working in industry. A mentor is someone from whom you learn, and who in turn becomes so interested in you that he or she will frequently sponsor you for various things. A mentor will help expand your skills and may participate in your intellectual development. And, very importantly, many mentors have extremely helpful job contacts. Such individuals are usually good sounding boards as job considerations develop. As such, the mentor is usually a combination parent, brother or sister, and friend.

Continue to develop mentor relationships as you move through the business world. Mentors not only frequently facilitate your career entry, but also often learn about new openings or know key people in companies or industries which may be of later interest. Make your mentor an integral part of your career strategy and job search.

And if by chance you do not have a mentor, start down the mentoring path as soon as you join your new company. Before you know it, you will be a mentor to someone yourself.

What Businesses Want and What You Have to Offer

Even in this age of greater functional specialization, most companies want executives with the potential to run a total business, develop an organization, think conceptually in terms of research and development, and inspire an organization. Companies want MBAs to become leaders with a broad vision. They want future vice-presidents of finance, not managers of accounts payable. They want future merchandising vice-presidents, not fashion dress buyers. Even in times of immediate demands on profits, companies think of MBAs as a future investment. MBAs represent prospective top management.

It is well known that work experience is desirable prior to entering an MBA program. It is equally well known that MBA graduates receive more consideration for better positions when they have some prior work experience. If you have had none, you should make every effort to acquire some while you are in the MBA program through internships, summer work, part-time work, and live company consulting projects in courses.

While you should be an overall generalist, you'll also need strong functional know-how with numbers, financial expertise, and marketing management to fulfill the assignments in most entry-level positions, so that your generalist capabilities can ultimately be utilized. It is almost impossible to become a broad management person without knowing and successfully performing the nuts and bolts of the business. It is even more important to have these capabilities when you are obtaining your MBA degree from a school with little prominence. A list of schools with accredited MBA programs is indicated in Appendix I.

Geographic Location

Determine the geographic area you desire, and be assured that there are many good job opportunities available there. Of course, there are some geographic areas that have more potential than others. For example, right now the Southwest offers more growth than the Northeast. Yet many MBAs successfully locate in Boston, New York, Philadelphia, Hartford, and Washington, D.C. Some want to stay in their home city or where they went to college or graduate school. Others desire a particular city for reasons like the weather, the skiing, the seashore, or the cultural life.

Some MBAs have no idea where they wish to locate, and some make the mistake of desiring a particular location but not balancing this with the attractiveness (or lack thereof) of the position. Consider a location, too, because of the unemployment or competition there. There are statistics available for each particular area or city—

which you can obtain from the library—that list companies needing MBAs. If you can afford to make a preliminary visit, fine. If not, get detailed information on the cities from AAA literature, travel books, and by contacting better business bureaus and universities in that city.

Conduct Informational Interviews

As a way of finding out more about job opportunities and career paths, set up some interviews strictly to obtain information. These informational interviews can be very relaxed affairs. Although you are indeed on display, it is not the same as interviewing for a position. Informational interviews can be used to find out about certain industries and companies, company managements, the future of certain types of business, and how comfortable you feel in certain environments—in short, almost anything you wish to pursue. Of course, you must know what you want to find out about, and you must be brief.

Business people are often willing to be interviewed. Many want to help new recruits, and they get great ego gratification from these interviews. Finally, some executives are constantly looking for potentially strong junior executives for their companies. You should always remember that while this meeting is for informational purposes, you are still on display. You will be looked at very carefully, therefore you are in a unique position to make an important and positive impression. You may wish to return to that same company later on as a serious job applicant. It's an opportunity to leave a very positive impression without the heavy pressure of an actual interview.

Make a list of the firms you want to interview. Then find out the name of the most appropriate person in each firm to see. This can be accomplished by calling the company directly. Other leads can be obtained from business faculty, the MBA placement office, family, and friends. Referral interviews probably mean warmer receptions, and you can usually see more people this way, too. On the other hand, the direct route is by far the shorter one. In addition, the direct approach takes some assertiveness and will build your interviewing confidence.

You'll probably have more names than you need by the time you're finished. Be sure in compiling the list of companies and people that you develop a group of contacts that is representative of the types of situations in which you are interested. Some other situations should also be included for exploratory purposes.

Develop a cover letter similar to the one illustrated on page 51. Send out the letters, then follow up with a telephone call a week or so later to establish an appointment. After your appointment, send a thank-you letter.

You should approach an informational interview looking as you would for a regular job interview—that is, dress appropriately. Find out as much about the company as possible beforehand, just as you would for a regular interview. Know what you're going to ask. If you wish, carry notes with you and feel comfortable about taking notes during the interview. Be open to questions. *Never* leave a résumé during an informational interview—this would violate your invitation. You can always send a résumé, if requested, with the thank-you note. Immediately after the encounter, record all your impressions and any facts acquired during the interview.

Career-information interviews may be your best source of data on different career fields. Some of these interviews can be conducted on campus when companies visit, and you can combine these with regular interviews or sometimes have a separate career information time. The latter has to be planned well in advance because company schedules on campus are usually full.

When conducting an informational interview on career areas, be prepared to ask specific questions. You want to learn as much as you can in a short time. You can even give the person a prepared list of questions. Some of the following questions can be used to help determine the career area:

1. What do you do during a regular day's work?

2. What interests you most about your job?

3. Do you find any portion of your work boring? Why or why not?

4. What has been your career path?

5. How long have you been working in your career path? Where do you expect it to lead?

6. Are there other career paths into which you can transfer?

7. What prerequisites did you have to fulfill to get where you are?

8. Is there any academic concentration which would be particularly helpful?

9. What type of training accompanies this job?

10. Are you an MBA? Are there other (or any) MBAs in this career path in your company?

11. What is the salary range for each level in this field?

12. Would you undertake this career path again?

13. Is there a demand for people in this field? Is it a growing field?

14. Is the field changing? How do you keep up with the changes?

15. Is there a demand for MBAs in this field?

16. What do I have to do to get started in this career?

17. Are there any job descriptions and specifications available for some of the positions in this field?

There are a few important facts to remember when conducting such an interview. Be careful of the time, and do not overstay your welcome. *Be prepared to ask no more than six or seven questions.* Of course, have a few in reserve should there be time available.

Don't confine yourself to just one organization. Interview in competitive situations even if they don't interest you as much. You will find similar problems and learn even more about the company that is of most interest. Talk to other people in the industry; most people love to talk about their companies.

Keep all questions open-ended, and try to keep the interview moving smoothly. You want maximum information in the time allotted. Always ask questions you believe the company person can and is willing to answer.

Remember that you are asking for opinions and ideas. Always watch the person's reactions and emotional responses, as these will provide significant information.

Choosing an Industry and a Company

The choice of industry and—ultimately—company should whenever possible focus on growth opportunities. Unless you are firmly committed to a particular geographic area, industry, or company, flexibility should be the general rule, as some geographic areas and some industries have higher levels of competition than others. Table 4-1 lists the number of MBA degree recipients for each year between 1960 and 1981. While there were only 4,643 MBA degree recipients com-

TABLE 4-1 Business and Management Graduates

| Year | BACHELOR'S | | | MASTER'S | | |
	Male	Female	Total	Male	Female	Total
59–60	47,607	3,916	51,523	4,476	167	4,643
60–61	46,636	3,823	50,599	4,562	147	4,709
61–62	47,937	3,972	51,909	5,128	175	5,303
62–63	49,373	4,221	53,594	5,573	214	5,787
63–64	54,316	4,637	58,953	6,189	197	6,386
64–65	57,894	5,105	62,999	6,344	241	6,585
65–66	58,074	5,406	63,480	12,656	332	12,988
66–67	63,695	5,992	69,687	14,488	406	14,894
67–68	73,165	7,275	80,440	17,258	610	17,868
68–69	85,972	8,644	94,616	18,727	671	19,398
69–70	96,760	9,519	106,279	20,659	758	21,417
70–71	105,609	10,803	116,709	25,609	1,045	26,654
71–72	111,340	11,966	123,306	29,304	1,207	30,511
72–73	114,404	13,840	128,244	29,706	1,533	31,239
73–74	116,424	17,481	133,905	30,659	2,161	32,820
74–75	113,232	22,223	135,455	33,370	3,080	36,450
75–76	116,252	28,783	145,035	37,754	4,974	43,728
76–77	117,510	36,252	153,762	39,969	6,681	46,650
77–78	115,511	43,760	161,271	40,301	8,183	48,484
78–79	120,167	52,167	172,915	40,831	9,675	50,506
79–80	122,833	60,908	183,741	42,722	12,277	54,999
80–81	127,070	73,806	200,876	43,505	14,513	58,018

SOURCE: National Center for Education Statistics "Earned Degrees Conferred"

peting for the available jobs in 1960, this number escalated to 21,417 in 1970 and reached 58,018 in 1981. New MBA programs are being developed every day and present ones are increasing in enrollment, so the number of MBA recipients will continue to increase in the foreseeable future.

Of course not all recipients are of equal qualifications. Part of the competition depends on the school granting the degree, but MBA jobs will become more competitive, growing ever more so each year. Your best advantage is knowing what you want and going after it in a structured way.

In order to optimize your choice of industries and companies, follow the procedures outlined here to greatly facilitate this time-consuming yet important task.

Develop a preliminary list of companies and industries in which you are currently interested. Conduct library research to find recent articles on these companies and industries by checking the *Business Periodicals Index* in your School of Management Library. Look for articles published during the last three to five years. The index will point you to pertinent articles in such journals as *Business Week*, *Fortune*, and the *Wall Street Journal*. Write these references on 3 × 5 index cards, one reference to a card. Follow up on the most promising ones immediately, and file the rest for the future. (You will want to know everything about the companies that invite you to interview; these references will lead you to articles you can read later. Analyze the information you gather, then narrow down the possibilities by developing a target list of organizations.

For each name on your target list, obtain the names, exact titles, addresses, and telephone numbers of personnel officers and functional line managers, such as the vice-president of marketing or the vice-president of finance. While this information is often available in some of the sources described in the next paragraph, sometimes the most current information can be obtained by a telephone call to the organization.

Conduct an extensive search through all available source materials to secure information on your targeted companies. Some of the best materials include:

College Placement Annual

Annual reports

10K Reports

Dun & Bradstreet's *Million Dollar Directory*

Dun & Bradstreet's *Middle Market Directory*

Forbes magazine, annual industry report issue

Advertising Age, annual review of top 100 advertisers

Standard Directory of Advertisers

Poor's Directory of Corporations, Directors & Executives

Thomas' Register

Funk and Scott Indexes

New England magazine

Directory of New England Manufacturers

AMBA Annual Employment Guide

Telephone directories

In addition to these sources, the career center or placement ɔffice should have the following:

Information on managerial careers

AMBA Newsletters and *Annual Guides*

Information on individual firms

Annual reports

Current articles

Newspaper clippings

This research can be greatly reduced if you divide the work among other MBAs whose career interests are similar to yours. Duplicate the materials collected and exchange them, thus reducing the amount of time you have to spend on the critical information-gathering phase. You can then use even more time in developing your job campaign.

Some valuable but difficult-to-obtain information includes an examination of the company's philosophy (structured vs. unstructured approach); entry-level management titles; names of MBA contacts within the organization; and an estimate of the number of MBAs hired for entry-level management positions each year. While this information can be far from exact, it will indicate dramatic differences among the personnel requirements of different companies as well as reveal the organizational hierarchy of each company.

Obtain as much knowledge as possible on the training philosophy of each company. Some companies have very structured training, and feel that their training program is equivalent to obtaining a second MBA. While competition is fierce in these training programs, the MBAs who do well are considered the "hottest management prospects around." Experience in such a structured training program leads to vast opportunities outside the company in addition to a fast track possibility within the company.

Some critics of this type of structured training say that this environment causes MBAs to be pigeonholed. In other words, they feel MBAs learn to work on only a small piece of any problem and therefore can't make a real impact on the organization. An unstructured training environment can afford a new MBA broader exposure and a chance to make more general decisions that have a tangible impact on the company. This, they claim, develops better management skills.

The main disadvantage of unstructured training is that learning is not as in-depth and the management techniques employed are often not as sophisticated. MBAs who favor an unstructured environment need to be self-starters.

Consider a scale of 1 to 3 which describes the training environment at various companies. On the scale, 1 represents a structured environment, 3 an unstructured one. Use this scale to determine the correct training environment for yourself. Determine a company's position on the scale during the interview. If you understand the company and its training philosophy, you will be a step ahead of other MBAs searching for management positions.

Table 4-2 gives an example of some hard-to-find information on twenty top consumer package goods companies. This is the type of information you should assemble for all the companies that interest you.

TABLE 4-2 Employment Facts on 20 Typical Companies

Company & Address	Training Environment Rating[a]	Entry-Level Title
BRISTOL-MYERS COMPANY 345 Park Avenue New York, NY 10022	2	Asst. Product Mgr.
CLAIROL, INC. (SUB. BRISTOL-MEYERS) 345 Park Avenue New York, NY 10022	2	Asst. Product Mgr.
DRACKETT COMPANY (SUB. BRISTOL-MEYER) 5020 Spring Grove Ave. Cincinnati, OH 45232	3	Asst. Brand Mgr.
CARNATION COMPANY 5045 Wilshire Blvd. Los Angeles, CA 90036	2	Brand Mgt. Trainee
COLGATE PALMOLIVE 300 Park Avenue New York, NY 10022	1	Asst. Product Mgr.
GENERAL FOODS 250 North Street White Plains, NY 10625	1	Asst. Product Mgr.
GENERAL MILLS General Offices Post Office Box 1113 Minneapolis, MN 55440	1	Marketing Asst.
GILLETTE COMPANY Prudential Tower Bldg. Boston, MA 02199	2	Asst. Product Mgr.
GREEN GIANT COMPANY Hazeltine Gates Chasta, MI 55318	3	Marketing Asst.
HALLMARK CARDS 25th and McGee Kansas City, MO 64108	3	Line Planner

a. In the training environment a "1" stands for the best and a "2" next best.
b. These figures represent an educated guess based on first-hand interviewing experience of MBAs in the spring of 1978. The estimates are figured per year. This usually means two recruiting periods for the companies that recruit a large number of entry-level MBAs for product management positions; one in the spring and one in the fall.

MBA Contact(s)	Est. # of MBAs Hired/Yr. into Product Mgt.[b]	Organizational Hierarchy[c]
Robert J. Stack Mgr. Corp. Staffing	1–2	Asst. Product Mgr. Assoc. Product Mgr. Product Group Manager
William Leonard Personnel Mgr.	6–7	Asst. Product Mgr. Assoc. Product Mgr. Product Group Mgr.
Bruce York Employment Mgr.	2–3	Asst. Brand Mgr. Brand Mgr. Group Product Mgr.
Frank Slohn Mgr. of Recruitment	3–4	Brand Mgt. Trainee Assoc. Brand Mgr. Brand Manager
J. Herbert Wise Director Human Resource Devel.	8–10	Asst. Product Mgr. Assoc. Product Mgr. Product Manager
James Kennedy Mgr. of Employment	25–35	Asst. Product Mgr. Assoc. Product Mgr. Product Manager Product Group Mgr. Category Manager
Robert Newsome Mgr. of Recruitment	20–30	Marketing Assistant Asst. Product Manager Product Manager Marketing Director General Manager
Ed Blanchard College Relations	8–10	Asst. Product Mgr. Product Manager
Robert Lyngen Personnel Mgr.	1–2	Marketing Asst. Asst. Product Mgr. Product Mgr.
James Large College Relations	2–3	Line Planner Asst. Product Mgr. Product Line Mgr.

c. First title given is entry-level position.
SOURCE: Most of the contents of this table are a part of a report: David M. Walsh, Rob Sligh, Michael Wesnofske, "Job Search Model for Product Management: Package Goods," submitted in partial fulfillment for a class in Market Analysis and Models, Boston College, Graduate School of Management, May 1, 1978.

TABLE 4-2 Employment Facts on 20 Typical Companies (*continued*)

Company & Address	Training Environment Rating[a]	Entry-Level Title
INTERNATIONAL MULTI-FOODS Eighth and Marquette Minneapolis, MN 44502	3	Asst. Prod. Mgr.
JOHNSON AND JOHNSON Personal Products Div. Milltown, NJ 08850	2	Asst. Product Mgr.
JOHNSON WAX World Headquarters Racine, Wisconsin 53403	2	Asst. Product Mgr.
KRAFT, INC. Retail Food Group 500 Peshtigo Court Chicago, IL 60690	2	Marketing Analyst
NESTLE COMPANY 100 Bloomingdale Road White Plains, NY 10605	2	Asst. Product Mgr.
PHILIP MORRIS 100 Park Avenue New York, NY 10017	3	Asst. Product Mgr.
PILLSBURY COMPANY 608 Second Ave., S Minneapolis, MN 53402	2	Asst. Product Mgr.
PROCTER AND GAMBLE CO. P.O. Box 599 Cincinnati, OH 60654	1	Brand Assistant
QUAKER OATS COMPANY Merchandise Mart Plaza Chicago, IL 60654	1	Asst. Brand Mgr.
STANDARD BRANDS 625 Madison Avenue New York, NY 10022	3	Asst. Product Mgr.

a. In the training environment a "1" stands for the best and a "2" next best.
b. These figures represent an educated guess based on first-hand interviewing experience of MBAs in the spring of 1978. The estimates are figured per year. This usually means two recruiting periods for the companies that recruit a large number of entry-level MBAs for product management positions; one in the spring and one in the fall.

CHOOSING AN INDUSTRY AND A COMPANY

MBA Contact(s)	Est. # of MBAs Hired/Yr. into Product Mgt.[b]	Organizational Hierarchy[c]
Gorden Sandbaken Dir. of Personnel	1–2	Asst. Product Mgr. Product Manager
Robert B. Miller Group Product Dir.	1–2	Asst. Product Mgr. Assoc. Product Mgr. Product Manager
Richard Meyers Employment Mgr.	3–4	Asst. Product Mgr. Assoc. Product Mgr. Product Manager Group Product Mgr.
Robert Clark VP—Marketing Info.	5–6	Marketing Analyst Asst. Marketing Mgr. Marketing Manager
C. J. Pelisson Mgr. of Employment	3–5	Asst. Product Mgr. Assoc. Product Mgr. Product Manager
John B. Burke Employment Mgr.	1–2	Asst. Product Mgr. Product Manager
Dave Smith Personnel Mgr. Consumer Products	1–2	Asst. Product Mgr. Assoc. Product Mgr. Product Manager
Henry Wilson, Jr. Mgr. Adv. Personnel	30–40	Brand Assistant Asst. Brand Mgr. Brand Manager Assoc. Adv. Mgr. Mgr. Adv. Dept. Division Manager
Wanda Zee Reimann Manager— Recruitment Grocery Products	8–12	Asst. Brand Mgr. Assoc. Brand Mgr. Brand Manager
Arthur Pearson VP—Marketing Services	1–2	Asst. Product Mgr. Product Manager

c. First title given is entry-level position.
SOURCE: Most of the contents of this table are a part of a report: David M. Walsh, Rob Sligh, Michael Wesnofske, "Job Search Model for Product Management: Package Goods," submitted in partial fulfillment for a class in Market Analysis and Models, Boston College, Graduate School of Management, May 1, 1978.

In Conclusion

You must have background information in order to decide on a company. It is necessary to know each firm's strengths and weaknesses, as well as its short- and long-term needs. Even more important, you need to determine the qualities and characteristics necessary for the available positions.

These needs or problems are not always large and difficult. They may even be readily apparent. However, don't try to teach the employer. You do not want to appear as a "know-it-all" from an MBA program. You want to find out what the company needs, and strike a chord that will prompt the company to conclude, "We need this person." If you have some specific ideas to suggest (and you frequently should have), don't make them too grandiose unless you really have something unusual.

How can you get a good feeling about a company? Start out by trying to understand the company: how it is organized, its strengths and weaknesses, its opportunities and threats. Is the company expanding? Why? What are the company's needs? If the company is on a plateau, what is needed to get it moving? If it is on a downward trend, what is needed to stem the tide? Where is the deadwood? If you are having a preliminary interview with a company which interests you, ask them about its problems. Everyone likes to discuss his or her problems.

Remember through this entire process that you are trying to match your education, experience, and ability to a company's needs. Don't discuss the problems of the world; concentrate on the company's problems, challenges, and opportunities.

COVER LETTER

3 Newbury Street
Boston, MA 02113
September 4, 1979

Mr. Phil McLaughlin, Vice President
Shawmut Bank of Boston
One Federal Street
Boston, MA 02211

Dear Mr. McLaughlin:

    I am currently an M.B.A. candidate at Boston College and will be receiving my degree in May, 1980. My concentration in the field of finance has led to the development of a keen interest in commercial banking.

    At the present time I am taking the preliminary steps necessary for a comprehensive job search. Your name was given to me by Mr. Gene Bronstein, Director of our Placement Office. In an effort to obtain information about the opportunities available in the area of commercial banking, I would welcome the chance to speak with you or anyone else in your organization that you may deem appropriate. This is not a request for an employment interview, but rather for a brief, informational session. My goal is to become more familiar with those aspects of commercial banking in general and your bank in particular which will enable me to make a more informed career choice.

    May I contact you by telephone during the week of September 10th so that we might arrange a convenient appointment? Thank you for your consideration of this request. I greatly appreciate any information that you may be able to provide.

Sincerely,

Mary C. Gallagher

c.c. Mr. Gene Bronstein

5

The Résumé

While a résumé is a requirement for any managerial position, it is seldom a benefit for either the MBA or the potential employer, and it will never alone result in a position. A *good* résumé is a sales tool that will open doors, and as such it should be an important consideration in your job campaign, receiving a significant amount of your time and effort. This important part of the job campaign should follow your identification of career possibilities and precede your actual campaign. It is essential that you understand the purpose of a résumé, know the information to include, and be aware of how to present that information in the most favorable way. Only then will your résumé open those doors for you.

Purpose of a Résumé

A résumé enables employers to become aware of your existence; it is very difficult (if not impossible) to obtain an interview without a résumé. But companies also use the résumé as a source of information about you, from which they draw additional information during the interview. The résumé is a picture of your qualifications in a concise, easy-to-read format that employers are used to. It saves everyone time, particularly the employer who would otherwise have to tie up hours during an interview asking factual questions about your background.

A résumé provides you also with an early review of your individual employability. The very acts of compiling the facts and organizing the résumé force you to look at yourself. The résumé helps you organize those facts of your education, your personal achievements, your professional experience, and your all-important accomplishments in a meaningful way. (Those facts also need to be updated annually as your career develops.) You'll learn about your goals and interests while you prepare your presentation for others' review, and if your goals need a little more focusing, the résumé may help you achieve that.

A résumé is also very valuable in business dealings such as buying businesses or obtaining consulting contracts. Often they are the basis for granting a business loan. In many dealings, you need to present your qualifications to others, and the résumé is a solid means of doing just that.

Frequently MBAs cannot obtain a desired interview because of a flaw in their résumé. A résumé is only as good as the time and effort you put into it. Given its critical role in your career, you should make it one of your priorities. It is no accident that this chapter on the résumé follows those on career decisions, or that it precedes a discussion of the job campaign itself. The résumé is really a very simple document to prepare, once you have established your career strategy, but it is only one part of your total job campaign. Many MBAs become frustrated when preparing their résumés, primarily because they have not taken the time to develop an overall job strategy. Their situation is somewhat comparable to building a house without some type of foundation. Don't get hung up on preparing this simple (but important) document! Instead, make a maximum effort to develop your career strategy; your résumé will follow smoothly.

A résumé is a representation of your career plans and your achievements. It is a picture of you, and it can be as mechanical and boring or as exciting and innovative as you view your life. Remember the word *accomplishments*. While a résumé starts as a vehicle for self-evaluation, it finishes as a positive image of your achievements and aspirations. It should indicate that you have achieved. It should stress your positive traits.

Your résumé is the sales key for an interview, and should be a compelling reason for a company to hire you. As a sales tool, the résumé should tell a company, which will spend thousands of dollars on you if you are hired, that you can be of value to it. In effect, your résumé is a forceful and truthful piece of self-advertising designed to convince companies that you are worth a certain price. It is not dishonest to stress your pluses; no good advertisement highlights the negatives of a product.

A strongly written résumé is a great confidence-builder. It is a graphic representation of your impressive credentials. Since it is such an important document, you will want to write it very carefully and certainly not in haste. And since a résumé must reflect you, you should write it yourself. Don't fall into the trap of believing a résumé is so difficult that you need a ghost writer. Your résumé is a personal document, and only you can put into it what is necessary to convey you and your accomplishments. There are, of course, many sources of help in résumé preparation. This book will give you formats. The MBA placement office at your college will have other tips. Faculty members can provide some guidance. Your mentor is a good sounding board. Finally your peers, many of whom are going through the same procedures, can provide some practical experience. Put it all together into a winning résumé.

The Need for an Outstanding Résumé

MBAs do not have to be better than all other applicants; their résumés should just present them in a way that they appear better. Since companies can receive hundreds of résumés for a specific opening, you must prepare an outstanding advertising message in order to obtain one of the few interviews.

In a personal conversation you can make adjustments and test reactions, but in a written résumé every thought has to be precise and accurate.

In today's competitive MBA market, your résumé needs to be outstanding. An outstanding résumé is one that projects you as briefly as possible, as honestly as possible, as excitingly as possible, and in the best possible language. Finally, underscore the word *honest*! While a less than honest résumé may get you the interview and even the job, sooner or later this error will cause you problems in your career.

Résumé Particulars

There is no set length for a résumé. It should be as long as is necessary to convey your academic, professional, and personal credentials without becoming verbose. A few MBAs will need to write a résumé for a special job; these résumés tend to be longer because an individual's experience is specifically related to a job's specification. However, most beginning MBAs will have a résumé of one or two pages.

The language of the résumé must be personal and interesting. A company who will spend time and money on you wants to know all about you before they make a decision. You should use an approach that reads like an aggressive sales letter, with crisp, exciting words that reflect an individual's potential. While the jargon of the career field should be incorporated, avoid slang. Choose your words carefully, making sure each sentence has both direct meaning and implications that go beyond the obvious. Make an instant impression.

Your résumé should contain the following information:

1. Your vital statistics: Name, address (with zip code), and telephone number (with area code). Be sure to list telephone numbers where employers can easily reach you.

2. Your objective: While some MBAs include a statement of professional objective, others do not want to be tied down to just one goal, especially if many copies of the résumé are being printed and distributed to different types of employers. In this case, either use more than one résumé (which tends to be cumbersome) or incorporate the objective in your cover letter. (A cover letter may, however, get thrown away.) Be sure you phrase your objective in terms of your top abilities based on your experience and your accomplishments. You do not need to mention a specific job; in fact, it is probably better not to do so. General job categories such as "finance" or "marketing management" are fine. Whenever possible, mesh your objective with the needs of the targeted employer, and communicate the skills you are going to offer that employer.

3. Your qualifications: Provide a brief summary, usually at the beginning of the résumé, which highlights unusual qualifications in your educational background (for example, Phi Beta Kappa). Detail your work ex-

perience (unusual responsibility at an early age), interesting internships (helped run a U.S. Senator's campaign), special school projects where outside companies were involved (a study of computer operations in four department stores), and any special abilities and traits which would make you a highly regarded candidate. Also mention special awards received. These indicate high intellect, leadership potential, and motivation.

What are some things most companies consider valuable? One is if you have put yourself through college or through your MBA program; this indicates strong ambition. Another is if you have done unusually well academically, as this represents a strong desire for achievement. One MBA candidate who was responsible for 100 percent of her educational expenses also achieved a 3.4 grade point average (out of 4.0); she was advised simply to put on her résumé her name, address, telephone number, education, a statement of her academic accomplishment, and the indication that she had put herself through school. After a great deal of reluctance, she followed this advice and received invitations from each of the six companies receiving the résumés.

4. Your education record: Since this is an extremely important part of the recent graduate's résumé, it should appear at the beginning unless you have had substantial business experience. List the educational degrees received, the schools, and the dates, beginning with your MBA degree and working back in time. Indicate the name of any private preparatory school, if applicable, and always indicate a high class rank, honors, awards, and scholarships. If you have taken any courses that particularly relate to your job objective, mention these. For example, if you are interested in an investment banking house, note any courses you have taken in financial management, investments, corporate financial management, and mergers and acquisitions.

    Extracurricular activities are part of any educational experience, so if you have enough of them and they are important, include them. Research assistantships, teaching assistantships, officerships of graduate student organizations are all important. Summer work experience between first and second years of the MBA program is particularly interesting to a prospective company.

5. Your professional experience: Most MBAs have work experience; indeed some have extensive backgrounds in industry. For each company where you have worked, describe the nature of its business. Indicate the size of the company by highlighting the number of employees. Most important, describe your duties and your contributions to the business. When your experience includes more than one previous job, start with the most recent position and work back in time. Present your work history in a positive, businesslike manner, as is indicated in the following example:

> Responsible for restructuring the merchandise assortments for the menswear division; developed entirely new sales promotion program for this restructuring as well as executive staff to execute the program. The result was a 36 percent increase in profits.

As is indicated in this example, always stress your accomplishments. You can best develop this kind of material by asking yourself: What were the challenges of the position? How did I meet these challenges? And what were the results? If the position was an internship, describe why you took it, what you learned from it, and how you expect to apply this experience.

If you have changed careers or are looking to do so, indicate this, especially if the reason for your change is that you have noted a lack of opportunity in your present field or if you find the industry static. Such a change shows alertness and motivation. If you have had several jobs recently, you may need to explain why this has occurred to avoid being viewed as a job hopper.

6. Your military service: This should be mentioned particularly if you were a commissioned officer with leadership responsibility. If the military service was for an extended period, relate that experience in a way that will be of value to the prospective employer. Many service records are relevant and can strengthen résumés.

7. Your professional memberships: Mention any memberships in professional societies such as the American Management Association, the American Marketing Association, the American Society of Public Accountants, or other significant organizations in your field. These indicate additional knowledge, and that you will expend extra effort to expand your horizons.

8. Your community efforts: These are also important to some companies. Work in fund drives or membership on a board of directors for some charitable agency is looked upon favorably. Companies view people with such credentials as having well-rounded interests.

9. Your special certifications: A CPA, CLU, Licensed Engineer, Licensed Real Estate Broker, and R.N. should always be included. These represent accomplishment, so be sure they are noted.

10. Your patents and publications: These indicate creative thinking and should be fully described. If you have published any business materials or acted as a research assistant, be sure to so indicate. These show you have engaged in original thinking and have excellent verbal and writing skills.

11. Your personal data: It is desirable to mention certain personal considerations such as home ownership, number of children, marital status, and willingness to relocate. Also mention any extensive traveling you may have done. Make note of fluency in any foreign language; this may be valuable to companies who deal on an international scale. If you have had government security clearance, list it and specify the level. Civil

service grades should also be noted, particularly if you are seeking a government position.

Since being a member of a minority group can be an advantage in certain companies, this can be indicated.

You may also wish to include mention of any unusual hobbies or sports. If you have any sports awards, note these; if you led any teams in college, indicate these as an example of your leadership ability and potential.

Special letters of recommendation can be helpful but these are best incorporated in a summary page or in a summary paragraph at the conclusion of the résumé.

Omit aptitude and psychological test results from your résumé unless they reinforce your qualifications and accomplishments. Also omit reasons for leaving previous jobs unless you feel their inclusion will be particularly helpful or explanatory. This will rarely be the case, however. Remember the old adage, "Don't voluntarily put yourself down."

The extent you include personal information depends on how relevant it is and how comfortable you feel about having the items considered by prospective employers. While you may use a photograph if you think it is important, it certainly is not necessary.

Here are some tips for résumé preparation:

1. Be concise and relevant, yet complete.

2. Make the résumé easy to read.

3. Don't exaggerate or project slickness. Avoid gimmicks.

4. Avoid spelling errors and grammar mistakes.

5. Avoid a boastful or dishonest résumé. Be truthful but positive.

The following are twenty questions you should ask yourself

when preparing and evaluating your résumé. Use these as a checklist when drafting the résumé until you have your final version.

1.   Is your name, address, and telephone number included, at the top of the first page?

2.   Is your name at the top of every page?

3.   Have you included an objective? If not, do you have a reason for not doing so?

4.   Have you related your accomplishments to your objective in your summary paragraph if you have one?

5.   Have you indicated in your objective how you expect to help your employer?

6.   Have you emphasized results produced, challenging situations overcome, and significant achievements?

7.   Have you used quotes from supervisors and peers in praising your performances?

8.   Have you covered important aspects of your education including honors, high class rank, self-paid tuition, and leadership roles?

9.   If you have stated an objective, have you emphasized the functional area in which you seek employment and the type of job you want?

10.   Does your objective indicate what you can accomplish for your employer?

11.   Have you avoided any generalizations such as references to maturity and integrity?

12.   Have you emphasized strong personal attributes which indicate energy, competence, and strong interpersonal relationships?

13.   Is your grammar and spelling correct?

14. Do most sentences in your résumé start with action verbs such as *supervised, developed, planned,* and *achieved*?

15. Have you been too modest?

16. Have you been specific in describing your achievements, such as noting a 10 percent increase in sales, a 20 percent decrease in selling expense, or a 15 percent increase in profit?

17. Is your résumé attractive, interesting, and easy to read?

18. Does the résumé mention your willingness to relocate?

19. Have you included everything which will motivate an employer to respond to your résumé?

20. Does your résumé end with a flourish?

Types of Résumés

Although you have the data at your fingertips, you have to organize your background information into appropriate categories and group them in an attractive, logical way. An important aspect of this organization is selecting a résumé style.

There are a number of types of résumés that can be used. The most frequent type for MBAs who have limited job experience is the chronological style. It provides the best setting to emphasize achievements, while providing companies ample opportunity for evaluation. In a chronological résumé, the work experience is indicated in reverse order of happening, the last or present job being given first. Similarly, positions held in a particular company are also discussed in reverse chronological order, indicating the growth and development that occurred.

The chronological résumé should include your name, address, etc.; objective; educational background; business experience (name of each company, description of company, your responsibilities, your accomplishments in each job); military experience if any; extracurricular activities; accreditations as described previously; professional memberships; community activities; and hobbies. It may be one or more pages in length, but it should be concise, relevant, and exacting and should include only material that reflects your qualities and aspirations. Two examples of chronological résumés are indicated on pages 64–69.

A second type of résumé for MBAs with good business experience is a chronological résumé with a "summary page," an example of which is indicated on pages 70–73. The summary page highlights exciting facts in the MBA's background. While it is the first page of the résumé, don't write it until the résumé itself is completed. You want to base it on the facts in the résumé. The summary page should stimulate the company to want to know more about you; it should also give the reader a quick picture of you. Use a summary page to strengthen a weak résumé, however, don't use it if your résumé is unusually long.

The third type, the functional résumé, highlights your professional experience by function, such as marketing and sales experience, general supervisory and management experience, operations and production, and financial expertise. In this type of résumé, a chronological arrangement of events is not followed.

The functional résumé highlights your experience in the same way the summary page does, but it emphasizes your accomplishments not specific companies or jobs. Most employers are more interested in your accomplishments than in what companies you worked for, so the functional résumé is very useful when you have gaps in your employment history. The functional résumé is briefer than a chronological résumé and it is especially well regarded by recruiters.

Functional résumés are particularly useful for MBAs with supervisory experience in major facets of management, when they have diverse experience and accomplishments, and/or substantial accomplishments. This type of résumé is particularly useful for people who have had experience in selling or sales management, product or brand management, plant management, research and development, teaching, or educational administration. An example of a functional résumé is on pages 74–75.

A fourth type of résumé is the functional-by-company résumé. This style presents your history chronologically by company and it stresses your experience and accomplishments. It is one of the best types of résumé, but can only be used by managers with strong experience and with accomplishments over a relatively brief period of time. Two types of functional-by-company résumés are indicated on pages 76–79.

Some MBAs, particularly those seeking to enter the advertising or arts fields, use a fifth-type—the creative résumé. This type really does not have a structured format but rather takes shape depending on the needs of the MBA and the position desired. You develop the specific form and style, and the perception of the résumé depends to a large extent on the skill and creativity put into its development. Writers, artists, musicians, and entrepreneurs sometimes use this form. Remember, though, it must be creative and not garish or extreme. An example is indicated on page 80.

Finally, for MBAs wishing to disguise the length of employment, employment gaps, or job hopping, the accomplishment résumé may be the best format. The objective of this type is to obtain the interview and explain some of the problems in person.

An accomplishment résumé is composed of personal data; summary of qualifications; summary of accomplishments; a listing of employers without dates; a listing of military service without dates; educational background with dates; hobbies, professional memberships, community activities, and honors with dates. An example of such a résumé appears on pages 81–82.

CHRONOLOGICAL RÉSUMÉ #1

1550 Broad Street   (203) 619-4232
Hartford, CT

ALICE MOAB

Objective

INVESTMENT   Urban financial consulting; new
BANKING: issues; new business; financial
               services; research.

COMMERCIAL   Money market research; municipal
BANKING: lending, financial services.

Education

M.B.A. with honors Indiana University—Finance.
A.B. Magna Cum Laude University of Chicago—
English.

Personal

Age 32, married, dual-career couple, strongly
interested in all financial areas of the economy; will
relocate; reading and writing strong interests.

Experience and Accomplishments

1974–1980   CHARLES BOYER AND CO.,
               2 Smid Street, Hartford, CT

FINANCIAL ANALYST, Research Department for
Investment Banker and full-service retail brokerage.
Department handled approximately 50 new research
projects each year over the last five years. This effort
represented a volume of 300 million dollars.

Responsible for:
—member of team of three developing research on a
  wide range of consumer and industrial products.
—developed and helped present 52 research reports
  to corporate managements most of whom are part
  of the Fortune 500.

Responsibilities involved:
—gathering secondary data.
—planning primary research activities.
—analyzing data.
—writing detailed reports.
—presenting to corporate managements.

Accomplishments in the above responsibility:
—100 companies selected Charles Boyer and
  Company to participate in underwriting of issues.

1972–1974   CALVIN SMITH AND CO.,
              1 Jones Street, Providence, R.I.

BROKER, Retail stock issues.
—sold to company-supplied customers.
—developed own customer list.

Accomplishments in the above responsibility:
—become #1 retail broker in two years.
—offered bonus of $5,000 to remain with company.

Qualifications

—Motivated
—Strong interpersonal relations
—Good listener
—Adaptable
—Good manager under fire

Interests

—photography, specialty people
—challenge of mathematical games
—securities markets

References and further data on request.

CHRONOLOGICAL RÉSUMÉ #2

Daniel Lewis Young
54 Sheffield Road
Newtonville, Mass. 02160
(617) 772-4072

qualifications: motivated
                         responsible
                         sensitive
                         well organized
                         courageous
                         good listener

education: MBA, MSW Degrees, May 1982
                         Boston College, Chestnut Hill,
                            Mass.
                         Concentration in Graduate
                            School of Social Work
                         Management of Social Service
                            Agencies; concentration in
                            Graduate School of
                            Management-Finance

                         Bachelor of Arts Degree
                         Trinity College, Hartford, Conn.
                         Concentration in Psychology
                         Dean's List, graduated with
                            honors
                         President of Senior Class,
                            Trinity College

experience:

Sept/78-May/79   PHOTOGRAPHY EDITOR
                  Trinity College Yearbook,
                     Hartford, Conn.
                  Developed a photographic
                     strategy for a nationally
                     distributed yearbook.
                     Supervised staff of twenty
                     photographers.

Jan/79-May/79   INTERN COUNSELOR
                  Project: DETOUR, Groton,
                     Conn.
                  Successfully counselled a
                     juvenile offender who would
                     not talk with previous
                     therapists. Prevented a
                     second teenager from
                     committing suicide.

March/78-May/78   INTERN COUNSELOR/TUTOR
                  Main Street House, Noank,
                     Conn.
                  Initiated group therapy/
                     activity sessions. Was able to
                     involve withdrawn resident
                     who would not previously
                     participate.

Sept/77-March/78 INTERN THERAPIST
                  Seaside Regional Center,
                     Waterford, Conn.
                  Through play therapy, got five-
                     year-old to talk for the first
                     time. Prevented an
                     unadvisable marriage
                     between two retarded
                     residents. Learned and
                     administered psychological
                     tests.

June/73-August/75   SALESPERSON
Underground Camera,
   Cambridge, Norwood and
   Framingham, Mass.
Started as youngest employee.
   Became highly proficient
   and knowledgeable in
   photographic skills.

May/76-August/77   VOLUNTEER CLINICAL
   EDUCATOR
McLean Hospital,
   Psychoeducation Unit,
   Belmont, Mass.
Worked six hours a day with a
   psychotic twelve-year-old
   girl.

Jan/76-May/76   VOLUNTEER AGGRESSION
   COUNSELOR
Home Street Day Care Center,
   New London, Conn.
Challenged and prevented
   abuse of a student by an
   employee.
Controlled aggression in the
   students.

May/74-August/74   VOLUNTEER PLAY
   THERAPIST
Children's Hospital Medical
   Center, Boston, Mass.
Used bilingual skills in
   communicating with
   Hispanic patients.
Eased fears of being ill and
   hospitalized through play
   with the patients.

Oct/75-Feb/76   VOLUNTEER COUNSELOR
Waterford Country School,
    Quaker Hill, Conn.
Improved social behavior and
    communication skills of a
    previously abused nine-year-
    old girl.

July/74-Dec/74   VOLUNTEER TEACHER'S AIDE
Plowshare's Childcare
    Program, Newton, Mass.
Worked successfully with a
    child who had been involved
    in a difficult divorce
    situation.

interests: photography, specializing in
    people, animals and flowers
the mechanics of automobiles
the challenge of mathematical
    games
animals, especially their care
    and training

References and further data on request.

CHRONOLOGICAL RÉSUMÉ WITH SUMMARY PAGE

Résumé of
Nancy Ann O'Hare

OBJECTIVE

Product and Marketing Management

1. Directed strategic product, marketing and promotional plans for wine products resulting in 15% sales growth and product line earnings.

2. Developed and implemented strategic product and marketing plans for Israeli Liqueur Sabra resulting in a 54% increase in case sales and a 39% increase in product line earnings.

3. Financed 100% of M.B.A. Graduate School education and 50% of undergraduate education.

4. Evaluated by senior managers as a decisive leader, inspirational to subordinates and respected by customers. Winner of an SEI Outstanding Achievement Award.

RÉSUMÉ

Nancy Ann O'Hare
762 East 22nd Street
New York, NY 10062
Telephone (212) 357-7620

PROFESSIONAL
EXPERIENCE

9/78 - Present   JACK AND JILL SPIRITS GROUP
New York, NY
Associate Product Manager, Mateus
Wines, 9/80 - Present

Developed strategic marketing
plans. Achieved specific profit and
volume goals for Mateus products,
nationally marketed imported
wines with total sales in excess of
$45.5 million annually and over $8
million in annual AMP spending.
This position reports directly to the
Group Product Director.

Specific Achievements:
—Reversal of downward sales trend
  to grow 15% in sales and 14% in
  product line earnings during
  CY80.
—Directed development and
  introduction of a new television
  and merchandising campaign
  reflecting a change in strategy.
—Winner of three golden awards
  for the top animated commercial
  in the New York and Chicago
  International Film and TV
  Festivals.
—Developed a new direct mail
  marketing approach for product
  line for three national mailings.

Associate Product Manager, Imported Liqueurs, 6/79 - 9/80

Responsible for the development and implementation of strategic marketing plans and objectives for Israeli Sabra. Total sales $12 million with annual AMP expenditures of $3 million. This position reported directly to the Group Product Director.

Specific Achievements:
—39% increase in product line earnings and a 54% increase in case sales.
—Managed and developed two related new products.
—Winner of ANSEI Outstanding Achievement Award.
—Prepared and presented to top management quarterly competitive marketing analysis.

Assistant Product Manager, Brown Goods, 9/78 - 6/79

Responsibilities included analysis of category and market trends, directing and assisting in the implementation of marketing plans and objectives for Black Velvet, Black and White, and Yukon Jack.

8/77 - 8/78	**JOHNSON'S WAX** Marketing Research Analyst

Managed marketing and statistical services for laboratory and national taste test panels and the Product Development Group. Directed data analysis, concept testing and packaging testing. Managed special projects in consumer personality profiling, descriptive terminology and panel mailout techniques.

EDUCATION

MBA, Boston University
Concentration: Marketing
Graduate Research Assistant
President, MBA Class of 1977

AB, Tufts University
English, Cum Laude
Member of University Debating
   Team for three years

Financed 100% of graduate school education and 50% of undergraduate education

ADDITIONAL
EXPERIENCE

American Marketing Association
   Research Fellow
Burke Marketing Research Seminar
President, Student Chapter A.M.A.
Research Fellow, Marketing Science
   Institute, Cambridge, MA.

References and further data furnished on request.

FUNCTIONAL RÉSUMÉ

Lindsey Ann Hansen
100 Dell Street
Bryn Mawr, PA 42016
(466) 371-6251

OBJECTIVE

Sales Manager of a Consumer Good in a Multi-Product Company

SUMMARY OF QUALIFICATIONS

Experience as a sales representative in the women's apparel field responsible for fourteen million dollars worth of volume to department and specialty stores.

General Management—Advised top management regularly on sales trends and customer buying habits as well as retail sales trends. Used as an advisor by management on retail cooperative advertising programs.

Sales Training—Supervised six junior salespeople all of whom succeeded on the job. Consulted by V.P. sales regarding sales quotas and income incentives for sales reps.

Production—Well respected by company operations executives and used to coordinate sales and production plans.

Finance—Increased speed of accounts payable payments thus increasing cash flow by 8%.

For Further Data, Please Read On

LINDSEY ANN HANSEN

PROFESSIONAL HISTORY

1973-1980	The Charles Company	New York, NY
1971-1973	Leslie May Inc.	New York, NY

EDUCATION

1980 - 1982	M.B.A. with Honors, University of Michigan, Ann Arbor, Michigan
1967 - 1971	B.A., English, Magna Cum Laude, Barnard College, New York, New York

COMMUNITY ACTIVITIES

Member of Board of Directors - 92nd St. Y.M.C.A.
Member of Minister's Committee, Riverside Church,
  New York, NY
Volunteer - New York Hospital for Women

HONORS

M.B.A. Degree with Honors
B.A. Degree with Honors
Phi Beta Kappa at Barnard College
Winner of National Sales Award

HOBBIES

Tennis, golf, jazz and classical music, champion
bridge player

PERSONAL DATA

Single, excellent health and willing to relocate

References and Further Data on Request

FUNCTIONAL-BY-COMPANY RÉSUMÉ–PROFIT

14 Highland Street   (703) 244-3610
Newtonville, VA 23222

CHARLES DUNLOP

OBJECTIVE: Divisional Merchandise Manager of a
retail department or specialty store.

EXPERIENCE

Buyer 1978 - 1980
The Smith Company   Richmond, Virginia
Bought women's fashion accessories for a
department whose volume was 1½ million dollars
in five stores. Increased sales volume 18%, market
share 5% and net profit before taxes 21%. Became
known not only as a strong merchandiser but also a
respected controller of expenses.

Assistant Buyer 1976 - 1978
The Jones Company   Charlotte, North Carolina
Developed strong operational capability particularly
with regard to branch stores and helped buyer
increase merchandise turnover one turn.

Executive Training Program 1975 - 1976
The Jones Company   Charlotte, North Carolina
Selected to assist a vice president for merchandising
for six months.

EDUCATION

M.B.A. University of Virginia, Charlottesville, Virginia
B.A. History, University of North Carolina, Chapel Hill,
North Carolina, Cum Laude

LANGUAGES

Fluent in French and Italian.

PERSONAL DATA

Single, good health, willing to relocate.

REFERENCES

Available upon request.

FUNCTIONAL-BY-COMPANY RÉSUMÉ—NONPROFIT

10 First Street   (761) 266-1420
Rochester, New York 54615

RÉSUMÉ
OF
THERESA PAT BROWN

OBJECTIVE

Director of Social Service Agency
Seeking to increase its client loans, its funding and to
improve its efficiency

EDUCATION

M.S.W. Columbia University, Graduate School of
        Social Work
M.B.A. Columbia University, Graduate School of
        Business
        Both with high honors.
B.A.   University of Rochester, Sociology,
        Cum Laude

SUMMARY OF QUALIFICATIONS

Six years of social service work as a case worker and
administrative assistant.

HONORS

Named in Who's Who in Colleges and Universities,
1974 and 1972
Winner of Social Worker of the Year Award in
Rochester, New York

PUBLICATIONS

"The Psychological Effect of Medication on Children Under 10 Years Old," Rochester Social Worker, 1976.

"The Effect of Poor Emotional Health on Reading Scores of Ten Year Olds," Columbia University Social Worker, 1977.

ACCREDITATIONS

New York State Regents License No. 46312
Rochester Board of Education License No. 61253

PROFESSIONAL EXPERIENCE

1974 - 1980   Rochester Agency for Disturbed Children
Social Worker Assistant and Staff Assistant to Director of Agency.
Assisted M.S.W.A.C.S.B. with patients. Participated in home visits and family therapy. Handled all budgets for the Director resulting in 18% decrease in agency expense. Organized a fund-raising drive which raised $48,000 for the Agency.

COMMUNITY EXPERIENCES

Volunteer at Rochester Aid to the Blind
Volunteer at Rochester Memorial Hospital

HOBBIES

Champion Chess Player

PERSONAL DATA

Single and willing to relocate. Financed undergraduate and all graduate education with scholarships, loans and outside work efforts.

REFERENCES AND FURTHER DATA ON REQUEST

CREATIVE RÉSUMÉ

10 Smith Drive   (Home) (617) 361-9125
Cambridge, MA 02613

RÉSUMÉ
Dariene Johnson

OBJECTIVE

Creative Art Director in National Advertising Agency

EDUCATION

M.B.A. Boston College
B.A.   Boston University, School for the Arts

QUALIFICATIONS

Ten years of creative art experience all with the
same agency in advertising of consumer goods
products, handled layouts and supervised budgets.

Boston Globe said: "The most knowledgeable
        advertising in Boston"
Boston Magazine said: "One of the really bright
        futures in advertising"
President of Advertising Club of Boston says: "She
        will be President of a national agency"

PROFESSIONAL HISTORY

1970 - 1980   Executive artist and assistant budget
                director

PERSONAL DATA

Single, financed all education, and willing to relocate.

ACCOMPLISHMENT RÉSUMÉ

Peter Marino

52 Smith Street   Home (502) 361-2401
San Francisco, CA 24312

PRODUCTION AND OPERATIONS MANAGER

Eight years experience as Production Liaison,
Foreman, Production Scheduler with experience in
Planning and Controlling Budgets and Expediting
Production.

Experienced at coordinating sales, purchasing of raw
materials and expediting production runs.

Excellent in writing reports and strategic plans for a
multi-million dollar company.

Further Data Below

ACCOMPLISHMENTS:

Increased raw material inventory two times in four
years.

Helped supervise building of plant costing 14 million
dollars.

Devised new inventory system for raw materials
saving $19,000 annually.

Handled all union grievances and reduced those
going to factory general manager by 114%.

Responsible for training six foremen and forewomen.

Reduced workmen's compensation claims by 22% in
three years.

Helped increase production by 29% in three years.

The above accomplishments were achieved for
Sheffield Steel Corporation in San Francisco, CA.

EDUCATION

M.B.A. Stanford University
B.A. in Mathematics Stanford University. Financed all
education.

PERSONAL DATA

Married, no children, willing to relocate.

6

Reaching Employers— Getting Them to Notice You

A s explained in the previous chapter, your résumé is a summation of your skills and potential. After you've developed your résumé, you need to present it effectively to the companies you have identified as potential employers. There are a couple of methods of doing this, including sending the résumé with the traditional cover letter, accompanying it with a hand-written note, or using the résumé to develop a direct mail letter.

The Traditional Cover Letter

Most people feel that a cover letter should always be sent with the résumé. Some even go so far as to attach a cover letter when the résumé is being routed by a placement office. Others attach a cover letter when submitting résumés for interviews on campus. The traditional cover letter can be very effective in getting your résumé read and in obtaining an interview. But while a strong cover letter can lead to interviews, a poorly written one, even with an exciting résumé, can negatively influence that process. And when writing skills are a critical part of a position, the cover letter becomes even more important. Remember: it is much easier to write a good cover letter than to create an outstanding résumé; therefore don't undermine the effectiveness of your good résumé with a mediocre letter.

A good cover letter indicates different assets from those shown on a résumé. A good cover letter will:

- Illustrate your writing ability and show how professional your communication skills are.

- Demonstrate your thinking patterns and reasoning skills.

- Show how much you know about the employer and the industry.

- Reveal your motivation in approaching the specific company and point to how you can apply your skills to that firm.

- Explain further any ambiguous points in your résumé.

- Present additional views of your personality and character.

Treat the cover letter as an advertisement for yourself. It should be relevant to the position, sharply and attractively written, and designed to promote you as a product worth further evaluation. Take time to write an effective letter; do not labor over your résumé and then treat the cover letter in a perfunctory way.

Don't use the same letter for all the companies you contact. Given the many letters they receive, companies are uncanny at spotting the lack of personal touch. The letter should be a very personal statement about you, and should reflect your own style and feelings.

The cover letter must be addressed properly. It should always be sent to a specific person, because addressing it to an office indicates laziness and indifference. Obtain the name of the correct person by telephoning the company directly. It is usually better not to use secondary data to obtain the names because people change positions frequently and the data you use may not be current. Do not hesitate to call distant companies for the correct name. You have invested a great deal of time and money in your education and have great earning potential ahead. Invest also in your personal advertising program.

Address your letter according to standard business format, as is indicated below:

Mr. James Brown
Vice-President, Marketing
Show Forms, Inc.
10 Madison Ave.
New York, New York 10023

The opening paragraph of the cover letter should include pointed details about your MBA degree, when it was awarded, and from where. It should also mention what type of position you are looking for and what prompted you to write to this specific company. Finally, the opening paragraph should indicate any striking academic or business accomplishments. Make this paragraph catchy; it needs to attract the reader's attention and get him to read further.

The main portion of the letter should focus on making the sale. State briefly your abilities, your experience, or your special attributes which make you attractive for employment. Also freely make reference to your résumé or anything else you are enclosing. In this section you are trying to persuade the employer that you are worth an interview. Highlight facts about yourself that indicate future success in the company by elaborating on certain important specifics in the résumé. Above all, focus on *how* your expertise is going to satisfy that employer's needs.

The letter should close with a strong request for an interview, a date of availability, a thank-you, a closing such as "sincerely yours," and a typed and handwritten signature.

Since the style and appearance of the letter indicate your writing capabilities, it must be grammatically perfect and contain no misspellings. The language should be simple and direct. Avoid clichés and vague phrases. Also avoid vague descriptions such as "challenging opportunity" or "creative job." Above all, be concise. Edit the letter several times before typing the final version, and always wait a day or so before sending it out to make sure it sounds as good as the day it was written. Get someone who is objective to give you his or her comments.

You already have laid the foundation for your cover letter if you have done everything indicated in Chapters 2–5. You know what you want to do, you know the type of company you wish to join, and you know what aspects of your background will be attractive to that particular company. Write your letter as if you are talking to the employer face to face and briefly incorporate important information about the company you will have obtained from sales or profit data, new product releases, or news of organizational changes. If there is a specific reason for your interest in the company, such as a statement from someone in the industry or a faculty member, indicate this.

Cite special MBA electives, internships, and significant course projects; these usually are of real interest to a prospective employer. Also include unusual MBA faculty support; this is impressive for the MBA who has limited business experience. But don't bore the reader with too much detail; the letter is not an interview in writing.

Don't hesitate to refer to your résumé frequently in your cover letter. Use any salient accomplishments and other facts to excite an employer. Remember you are selling the most important product of all—yourself. Focus on your mutual needs and make a sales pitch for an interview.

Make sure the letter speaks for you in a warm, energetic fashion. Come across as someone who is agreeable as well as aggressive. While a cool tone is usually equated with professionalism, too cool a manner may indicate a lack of rapport. Enthusiasm is an important aspect in your letter, so convey it in a professional manner and relate it to an accomplishment.

On the other hand, treat the potential employer as a friendly adversary. Everything in the letter must be positive; the cover letter is not the place to discuss weaknesses. Stress only your positive personality traits and interpersonal skills as they relate to the needs of the employer. Remember the following:

1. Use standard business-letter format in almost all cases. For two examples of this format, see pages 90–91.

2. Always address your letter to the person who will make the employment decision.

3. Always indicate the job you are looking for. This can

be accompanied by an explanation of why you are writing to that particular company.

4. Display good writing skills.

5. Expand, whenever possible, important information contained in your résumé.

6. Ask for an interview and thank the employer afterwards.

7. Make the letter no more than one page long, usually about three paragraphs.

Also avoid the following:

1. Never write anything that can't be substantiated.

2. Do not be vague. Be sure you understand why you are writing to that company and, whenever possible, give the exact nature of the position desired.

3. Do not sound nervous or urgent in the request for an interview.

4. Do not include any personal, political, or economic philosophies.

5. Do not exaggerate; just cite specific accomplishments.

6. Do not send a "blind" letter; send it to a particular person.

7. Do not send a résumé by itself; accompany it with a cover letter (exceptions are discussed later in this chapter).

8. Do not neglect the company's needs; always tailor your cover letter to the needs of the company.

9. Do not end abruptly; always conclude by asking for an interview, as a salesperson would close by asking for an order.

10. Do not send a sloppy letter; always proofread carefully before mailing. Examine its appearance, grammar, and spelling.

Handwritten Notes

There is a small group of MBAs who feel that because cover letters are boring, tedious, and redundant, they should be used only when the needs and desires of the employer are known. Instead of a cover letter, they send a résumé with a handwritten note at the top indicating that they will call at a specific time for an interview. This is a personal and somewhat unusual method of obtaining an interview, and while it can be worthwhile for some MBAs, you must be comfortable in using this format. An example is indicated on page 92.

Sales Letters

Another approach is to send an advertising, sales, or broadcast letter about yourself to the presidents of the companies for which you want to work. You develop such an advertisement about yourself based on the accomplishments delineated in your résumé, and the resulting letter sells your accomplishments, your abilities, your business and educational background, and your objectives. These facts should be written in a believable, exciting, readable fashion. (See pages 93–98.)

Always send these letters to the presidents of the companies, referring by specific name, since the person in this position always thinks in long range, broader terms about new talent needed in running the business. This way you avoid becoming bogged down with less than top-level executives and especially bypass slow-working personnel departments. When you obtain an interview through this approach, it gives you additional self-confidence.

In developing these letters, you will have done most of the work by preparing your résumé. In the case of sales letters, however, you will not be including a résumé. You will not even be leaving the résumé following the interview. The résumé is sometimes submitted later for reinforcement. Therefore the sales letter on its own has to make you stand out as a business-getter, a profit-maker, a potential company president.

As with traditional cover letters, do not become preoccupied with yourself and your job needs. The company is interested in what you can do for it. Your hopes, objectives, and financial needs are very important to you, but initially they are secondary to the employer. That employer becomes interested in your wants only after it appears you will be an asset. Your letter, therefore, must be specific and well written. Do not give vague descriptions of your accomplishments. Whenever possible, use precise numbers and action verbs such as *increased, boosted,* and *reduced* to cite results of your work. Show you can thrive in a competitive atmosphere.

The sales letter method isn't for every MBA. Use it only when:

- You have the type of background which permits you to bypass the personnel department.

- You have the combination of business experience and MBA background which will be exciting to a senior-level company executive.

- You have qualifications appealing to one particular executive.

- A spot could specifically be developed for a person with your background. This is often the case in a small firm.

- Your approach could save the company the time and expense of making trips to MBA campuses.

Telephone Contacts

A few MBAs in recent years have decided to try yet another technique. They are confident of their ability to sell themselves over the telephone, and this is exactly what they do. They select about a dozen companies at a time, and try to sell their way to an interview. One MBA who adopted this strategy after disappointing mail results found himself talking to the president of a medium-sized corporation. The president became so interested that an immediate interview was arranged, and eventually a new position was created as assistant to the president. An MBA who feels comfortable with this approach should at least try it on a sample basis. Nothing ventured, nothing gained.

COVER LETTER #1

March 15, 1983

Mr. John Columbus
Reliance Manufacturing Company
16 Thatlher Lane
Birmingham, AL 73215

Dear Mr. Columbus:

I know you will be interested in what I have to say because I have an interesting background in Production and Finance as well as a recently acquired M.B.A. degree from a fine Graduate School of Business.

My professional experience includes Production Control work as well as Quality Control and Supervisory Responsibility. In addition, I have handled all manufacturing budgets and cash flow requirements for production requirements.

My M.B.A. degree, which I will receive in June, has trained me in the most sophisticated financial techniques being taught today.

I am enclosing my résumé, and since I plan to be in Birmingham the last week of April, I would very much like to visit with you.

I will call you within the next ten days to arrange a mutually convenient appointment.

Sincerely,

Eugene Bronstein

Enclosure

COVER LETTER #2

Mr. Richard Jones
18 Smith Street
Cambridge, MA 02139

March 5, 1983

Ms. Jane Conroy
Vice-President
Charles Schultze and Company
16 Peterson Street
Detroit, Michigan 43215

Dear Ms. Conroy:

I am graduating with an M.B.A. from the Harvard
Business School this June with strong exposure to
Financial Analysis, Financial Management and
Investment Banking. I also have spent three years
working in the Mergers Acquisitions field.

I plan to join an investment banking firm active in
the above field.

I am bright, highly motivated and I can be depended
upon to produce.

I will be in Detroit during the third week of April. I
would like to meet you and I'll plan on calling you
for an appointment in the next week or so. I look
forward to meeting you.

Sincerely,

Richard Jones

HANDWRITTEN NOTE TO BE ATTACHED
TO THE RÉSUMÉ

March 1, 1983

Mr. John Smith:

I know that you will find this résumé exciting and worthwhile studying carefully.

However, a spoken word in person is worth more than any written page.

Therefore, I feel it would be worthwhile for you to spend some time with me when I am in your city in May.

I'll call you for an appointment shortly.

Sincerely,
Nancy Ann O'Hare

SALES LETTER #1

10 Charles Lane
Philadelphia, PA 76312
(209) 462-1520

April 15, 1983

Mr. William Merkle
President
The Charles Corporation
16 Charles Place
New York, NY 10097

Dear Mr. Merkle:

Because of 13 years of marketing management
experience in the dentifrice business, having sold in
the field for five of those years and because I have
just earned my MBA, there is no question about my
being ready for upper middle management marketing
responsibility.

My accomplishments are:

—Over the last three years, I have increased
sales 26%.
—I have reorganized our sales staff and have
trained eight new sales representatives.
—I have developed a brand new sales training
program which has produced those reps and
will produce more.
—I have planned three advertising and sales
promotion campaigns.
—Four of my sales reps have been promoted to
new jobs within our corporation.
—I developed the first new sales training manual
in over a dozen years.

I am an innovator and a seeker of profitable
business.

I seek a position as director of marketing or general sales manager for a medium-sized corporation in the consumer goods field.

I will call you within the next two weeks to arrange a mutually convenient appointment. I look forward to meeting you.

Sincerely,

Robert D. Hisrich

SALES LETTER #2

Mr. Norman Glass
1 Terrace Road
San Diego, CA 36315

April 10, 1983

Mr. Curt Jerkins
17 Market Street
San Francisco, CA 63215

Dear Mr. Jerkins:

I believe real estate (the right kind) is still a
marvelous way to "grow" money.

I have been in this business for 10 years and am just
about to receive my M.B.A. (evening attendance)
from the University of California at San Diego.

Professionally, I have been a salesman, appraiser and
analyst. I have become very knowledgeable at
estimating the market value of income-producing
properties for investment purposes.

Several large companies and two non-profit groups
have used my work and recommendations to make
profitable real estate decisions.

A major national retail chain has used my work to
analyze regional shopping center possibilities in
California and Arizona and made their selection on
the basis of my recommendations.

Companies which have large sums to invest could
benefit from my work. The same would be true of
those companies seeking optimum sites for plants
and shopping centers.

I have a B.A. degree from Stanford University in English.

I am single and willing to relocate.

I think you will be interested in talking to me. I'll be in touch with you shortly.

Sincerely,

Norman Glass

SALES LETTER #3

Charles Ryen
10 Congress Street
Manchester, NH 20543

April 5, 1983

Mr. Charles Gaynor
Executive Vice President
National Crepe Company
One Federal Street
Boston, MA 02113

Dear Mr. Gaynor:

I have been employed in marketing and economic research work for a major consumer goods company for the last five years. I also will receive my M.B.A. degree in June which I have obtained while working by going evenings.

My experience includes financial analysis, territory analysis, advertising effectiveness and share of market studies.

I would now like to expand my contributions to the profitability of a business by developing a total market research responsibility.

Here are some specific examples of my accomplishments:

1. After conducting a market analysis and recommending a change in channel strategy sales increased 18% with an increase in profits of 8%.

2. After analyzing a research study, I recommended a change in promotion

techniques which resulted in a 6% increase in share of market.

3. Developed a new sales forecasting technique which helped reduce inventory levels by 11% thus improving cash flow by 8%.

Because these accomplishments were so well-received, I have repeatedly been recommended for promotion. However, the present organization of my company does not permit expansion of my responsibilities at this time.

I am 30 years old, married and will receive my M.B.A. in June from the University of New Hampshire. I speak German and Spanish and am willing to relocate.

I think it will be worthwhile for you to meet me. I'll call you for an appointment in the next week or so.

Sincerely,

Charles Ryen

7

The Job Campaign

W hile there is indeed no one best way for an MBA to find a job, the most effective technique is to carry on several different campaigns simultaneously. The multiple approach avoids the exhaustion and negative self-image that can develop when you try one after another approach to no avail. In this regard, direct mail works well because it does not conflict with other job-hunting activities. Even if you are employed, you can carry out a direct mail campaign during evenings and weekends.

Any job campaign requires preparation, and the better your preparation, the more effective your eventual selling effort. Preparation also builds your confidence, which in turn brings you offers of the best jobs. You've set your goals, you've determined what you want to do and where you want to do it, you've identified the industries and companies you want to reach and you've prepared your résumé. Now you are ready for the contest!

Record Keeping

Before implementing your campaign, establish a concise and systematic record-keeping system. By setting up a filing system at the

TABLE 7-1 A Card Index of People and Companies Approached

Company	Company Executive	
Address	Title	
Telephone	How approached	résumé-cover letter
		sales letter
		informational int
		telephone
		employment agency
		executive general agency
		network
		name
		address
		telephone
Record of contacts	Date contacted	
	Follow-up	

very beginning, dull as that process is, you will be able to keep on top of every aspect of your campaign as it develops.

For good records, set up an alphabetical card index of companies you contact and note the means of contact; keep a list of potential employers and other contacts as you find them; and organize a simple way of handling return mail. See Table 7-1 for an example of a suggested card index; allow enough room to fill in information as you collect it. Your prospect list should be an informal, but organized accumulation of names of people, companies, associations, friends, and faculty who may be helpful in your job quest. The return mail file is more than just the answers to your mailings. It is a permanent record of those who have responded in some way to your campaign, and these individuals may be worth contacting in the future. Although some may not work out right away, it may be advantageous to contact them periodically. Others you may want to be in touch with on a professional basis after you are employed.

Your record-keeping system will make you feel confident and professional, helping you avoid wasting time searching through disorganized material; you can instead operate as an executive.

Perhaps the most important reason for having a simple record-keeping system is to be ready for that company officer who, fascinated by your résumé, calls you one day and expects you to know who he is and what he does. He would be surprised and disappointed if you didn't, and this initial reaction could rapidly turn against you.

Campaign Costs

Your job campaign is going to cost money. Job hunting is expensive, especially when you do it intensively—on an organized basis and if you cover all the options. Remember that you are striving for substantial stakes, and think about how many years you plan on working and at what average salary. You will make a fairly large sum of money. Decide, therefore, to make one more investment in your future. Indeed, the job compaign will cost far less than your MBA education. Look at job-hunting costs in light of what you can afford and what you estimate may be needed to ensure success.

You will need some money to maintain your files. You will need money for printing résumés and cover or sales letters. You'll also need money to cover typing services, photocopying, and postage. If you have no one to take telephone messages, you will need a telephone answering service or answering machine. Be sure also to set aside money for lunches, taxicabs, and parking fees. Everything in your campaign should be first class, since it represents what you think of yourself, and your image is extremely important.

In addition, there is the expense for clothing—an item you can continue to use after you secure the job. You are really packaging yourself through your clothes, and you have to look sharp to really feel sharp. It would even be good if you felt a little elitist. Make sure your clothing is relatively new, the right colors (blue or gray), and of the best quality. Also, you must have stylish accessories. And the correct clothing and accessories are important for both men and women. If you have any doubts, see the most knowledgeable salesperson in your favorite store or ask for the fashion coordinator. Remember: the person interviewing you will be evaluating you as a total package, including your appearance.

Some MBAs will take their job campaigns to other cities, but, except for such long-distance travel, your campaign should not cost more than $600. This is a small cost in light of your educational investment and when compared to the potentially higher starting salary you could obtain through a good campaign.

Basics of a Campaign

Most MBAs hesitate employing a direct mail campaign because they have heard that the response rate is extremely low. It is then suggested that this occurs because the résumés are so finely screened that they never reach the appropriate executives. While it is true that the number of jobs obtained through this method is low (as a percentage of the volume of correspondence), nevertheless a direct mail campaign can be very effective if conducted properly. The results of such an approach depend a great deal on the basics of your campaign: having a good mailing list, directing the résumé to the appropriate recipient, and sending a powerful letter.

Usually the best starting point to develop a mailing list, particularly for those MBAs currently employed, is your own knowledge or a friend's or acquaintance's knowledge of the trade or industry. But often, particularly for MBAs without work experience, these means are either too limited or virtually nonexistent. If the latter is your case, you can develop a larger list by using the resources of a good business library or by purchasing a commercial list, which was discussed in Chapter 4.

Obviously the major problem with a commercial list is that it has little or no information on individual companies. Since you are actually selling yourself as a product, it is imperative that you know the essential points about the company to receive your letter. Obtain this information from the company's advertising, *Standard and Poor's*, *Moody's*, *Thomas Register of American Manufacturers*, *Editor and Publisher*, *Fortune's Plant and Product Directory*, *Wall Street Journal*, and company's Annual Reports and 10K reports. The more specific and knowledgeable you can be about the company and its operations, the greater your odds of securing an interview.

Once you develop the mailing list and target the companies for correspondence, make certain your letter reaches the appropriate person in each company. Of course exactly who this person is depends on the company's organizational structure and the position you are seeking. It will usually be necessary to write to two individuals in each company—the personnel manager in charge of MBA and/or executive recruiting and the functional area manager. When in doubt, always send the letter to the *higher* ranking manager or the president. As previously mentioned, a letter can readily be referred down the organizational structure, but movement up is far less likely. When there are two or more divisions, send a letter to the functional area manager in each. For example, while the division of one company hired an MBA who approached that division directly, other MBAs who had written the corporate headquarters or a different division were given no encouragement. In that instance, only those letters received directly by the specific division had favorable results, because that was where the opening was and company policy placed recruiting and hiring power with division managers. On the other hand, in smaller companies the manager may hold several positions.

But how do you go about getting a specific name to send the letter to? There are two ways: to call the company and ask, or to check various directories. The first method is simple. Telephone and ask the name of the person in charge of the area in which you are interested, and you'll get the answer immediately. Do not hesitate employing this tactic since such inquiries are routine. If the secretary answering does not know or if it is corporate policy not to give out such information at the switchboard, then ask to speak to the person's secretary, who will probably give you the name. In the unusual case where it is corporate policy not to give out that information at all, listen carefully to the way the secretary answers. From hearing "Mr. or Ms. Nelly's office," you will have the name anyway. This problem can occur more in what companies consider sensitive areas such as research and development than in the typical line areas. If telephoning is prohibitive because of the costs (though, as previously mentioned, cost should not be an inhibitor in a job campaign), then send a letter to the personnel department to produce the same information. Bear in mind, however, that return correspondence is often not forthcoming or can take two weeks or more since it is not given priority.

You can also obtain the names of individuals by referring to published directories. For example, Dun and Bradstreet's *Million Dollar Directory* gives the names of all company officers in corporate and functional areas for firms of $1 million or more. Similar directories are available for other size companies. In addition, many industries have trade directories indicating the names of functional managers. This method is slightly less reliable than the first, however, because these directories are often outdated as soon as they are published.

Once all this information has been obtained, use it to advantage in the cover letter. Cover letters are discussed in the previous chapter, but a few additional comments are of value here. The cover letter in the job campaign has *one* purpose: to obtain a job interview. Use it to arouse interest in you. And be sure you do it neatly and concisely.

Targeted versus Hit or Miss

There are basically two types of direct mail campaigns: the rifle and the shotgun. To use the rifle, or targeted, campaign you compile a list of employers who frequently have openings in a specific area of interest, and you aim your cover letters at these specific targets. In the shotgun, or hit-or-miss, campaign, you mail letters to many firms hoping to stumble upon openings. In this latter campaign, your cover letters are similar to form letters with a few variations.

If you have a specific career such as international banking investments, product manager, or marketing research, you should conduct a direct campaign exclusively. Develop a target list of no more than twenty organizations, and spend time writing personalized and strategic letters for each. You might use some common paragraphs, but the overall thrust is to send a unique letter to each organization.

If you have a more general career goal, such as corporate finance or marketing management, develop two target lists: a high-priority list of ten firms and a low-priority one of forty. One graduating MBA employing this technique spent 80 percent of his effort on 20 percent of the mailings—his high priority list. In other words, he concentrated his effort on the firms in which he was most interested, but still covered a broad spectrum of backup firms. College placement officers report that the typical response to a normal 100-letter campaign is only about 4 percent or 5 percent. But by employing the above 80/20 technique, you may increase the positive response rate in your campaign to well over 20 percent.

To play it safe, one graduating MBA decided on a two-tier strategy. He was seeking a job in product management with a major consumer package goods company, and he used a targeted approach with a hit-or-miss approach as a back-up.* The results, indicated in Tables 7-2 and 7-3 respectively, illustrate that an MBA who uses only the hit-or-miss approach is just spinning wheels. This may be difficult to accept, especially for a student who wishes to conduct a thorough job campaign, however the reasons for the increased probability are evident. One of the first things the company will want to know is: Are you really serious about the specific position for which you are applying? That you have enough good reasons for your interest in the particular area is essential but not enough. Often they require tangible examples of your interest. For example, in the case of the product management career in the consumer packaged goods industry, the MBA often responded to the question of interest by saying: "As a matter of fact later this week I'll be in Minneapolis to see three of the

---

* *This example was part of an unpublished paper prepared for a class in market analysis and models—David M. Walsh, Rob Sleish, and Michael Wesnofske, "Job Search Model," unpublished paper, Boston College.*

TABLE 7-2 The Target Approach

Percentage of Companies Contacted	Number of Companies	Information
100	26	These top companies were contacted through letters and follow up telephone calls. Two were not packaged goods companies—however, this is an ill advised deviation from the plan. The candidate offered to visit the companies at his own expense to discuss opportunities in product management.
65	17	These companies agreed to see the candidate. The candidate interviewed with an average of 2.3 people the first time around, typically talking with at least one functional marketing person. The interview length averaged one hour.
11.5	3	These companies invited the candidate back for second interviews before the candidate's self-imposed cutoff of April 1.
11.5	3	Three companies extended offers to the candidate.

TABLE 7-3 Hit or Miss Approach

Percentage of Companies Contacted	Number of Companies	Information
100	129	These letters with typed names and addresses went out on January 1 to companies listed in the M.B.A. employment manual who were thought to have marketing related possibilities.
7	9	These companies expressed interest in setting up interviews.
1.5	2	These companies were evaluated by the M.B.A. as worth an initial interview.
0	0	These companies warranted further consideration after completing the first interview.

top packaged goods companies about opportunities in product management." As you get more and more adept at interviewing, you may want to discuss briefly how the functional area varies in opportunity and scope from one firm to another. This knowledge not only indicates your interest in the particular position but simultaneously implies that other firms are considering you as well. Remember, firms are just as interested in your ability to *achieve* your objectives as they are in those objectives themselves.

The targeted approach should achieve three broad objectives: to maximize the synergistic effects of interviewing many companies for the same type of job; to avoid wasting valuable time interviewing with companies that are on your "second string"; and to let the companies know that you have a serious commitment to the career. The direct approach is the most effective means of attaining these objectives.

One general objection to this technique is often discussed. The candidate may ask, "What if I am unsure about what I want to do?" You *must* make a career choice well in advance to obtain a top position. During the eight months prior to work, do your homework on industries and different jobs. The penalty for poor planning and indecisiveness may be either *under*employment or *un*employment.

Timing

One basic ingredient often overlooked in the campaign strategy is accurate timing. Graduating MBAs should begin a direct mail campaign at least five months prior to their anticipated graduation. This means that your résumé should be in final form and in the printer's hands no later than six months before graduation.

Experience indicates that functional managers have fewer demands on their time during the middle of the work week, and that they are more receptive to inquiries from MBAs at that time. Therefore Mondays and Fridays are not the ideal days to have your résumé and cover letter arrive on the manager's desk. If possible, schedule your mailings to arrive mid-week. As a general rule, have résumés arrive two days before you call the employer to set up an interview or five to ten workdays prior to visiting an out-of-town organization.

In addition, after deciding on the cities and companies you will visit, you must determine the best scheduling of appointments. You may want to plan the trips during vacation periods. Keep in mind, though, that being early in the interviewing season is at worst an inconvenience—you may have to go through an extra step in the interviewing process—but being late can be fatal. Top companies interview in January and February. Those candidates who are definitely wanted after the first interview are invited back in late February and March for second interviews, and are offered jobs five to ten days following the second interview.

Since companies often make three offers to get one candidate, there is indeed some uncertainty as to whether they will fill the open positions during this first round of interviews. Therefore, the companies keep a supplementary list of very competent MBAs who may be invited back in April for second interviews if the company is unsuccessful in attracting its first choices. You should start early enough to make the top list of candidates of at least some of the companies.

Travel to Other Cities

Although many companies come to the campus to interview, you should consider traveling to the corporate headquarters. There are several advantages:

- 🐾 You'll interview in the context of the organizational environment.

- 🐾 You'll accelerate the weeding out process to find which companies fit your criteria and which don't.

- 🐾 You'll be able to allow more time for the actual interview. Most on-campus interviews last 30 minutes while interviews at corporate headquarters usually last 60 minutes.

- 🐾 You'll see more than one person during the first contact phase with the company.

- 🐾 You'll impress the company with your enthusiasm for the job and ability to plan and execute a well-run job campaign.

A travel agenda requires a great deal of planning and organizing. First you must identify target cities in which there is a high concentration of companies with the position you desire. You must budget a certain amount of money for your trip and maximize the number of companies visited within your budget.

In setting up a tentative schedule for travel, plan on visiting two companies per day. Since the objective is to see two or three people in each company, allocate enough time to each company, plus enough time for lunch and for travel between the first and second company. Table 7-4 is an example of a schedule organized by the MBA searching for the product management position in a consumer packaged goods firm previously discussed. While the original schedule was certain to change, at least the MBA had a tentative date to include in letters to each company. This student received a 91 percent favorable response from Midwest companies. For the same MBA, a similar plan targeted at New York, New Jersey, and Connecticut produced only a 47 percent favorable response. You may want to set up alternatives in anticipation of some rejections. For instance, if you cannot get an interview with Quaker Oats in Chicago, you may wish to contact Beatrice Foods. Since scheduling is a difficult juggling act, begin at least a month ahead, and preferably two months, to allow time for changes.

The first step in scheduling a trip is to write to the appropriate companies. Send your letters to the correct persons and include a promise to follow up with a telephone call "the week of December 7," for instance. Anticipate some difficulties in getting through to someone at the company. Usually your letter has been referred to

TABLE 7-4 Sample Travel Schedule

MINNEAPOLIS			
Monday	January 5	Morning	Green Giant
		Afternoon	Pillsbury
Tuesday	January 6	Morning	International MultiFoods
		Afternoon	General Mills
CHICAGO			
Wednesday	January 7	Morning	Swift Foods
		Afternoon	Kraft
Thursday	January 8	Morning	Quaker Oats
		Afternoon	Alberto Culver
CINCINNATI			
Friday	January 9	Morning	Procter and Gamble
		Afternoon	Drackett

someone else, and the exchange between you and the secretary is likely to follow these steps:

1. You ask to speak with the person to whom you sent the letter.

2. The secretary mentions that that person is in a meeting. The secretary then asks if she can help.

3. You state the reason for the call and suggest that the letter may have been referred to someone else.

4. The secretary checks and finds that the letter has been referred to someone else and offers to connect you with that person.

5. Before the secretary makes the connection, ask for the correct spelling of the person's name, his or her title, and telephone number (in case you're disconnected). Record these in your file.

6. The next person will also have a secretary who will probably ask to take a message. Politely make sure that the individual did indeed receive the letter, making reference to the person in the company who had done the referring. In addition, make sure the new individual is the correct person to talk with after all.

7. After the secretary takes the message, ask when to expect a return telephone call. Record all information regarding telephone calls in your file.

The cost of the travel plan is of course "front end loaded." In other words, you incur costs now in anticipation of a higher return later. Table 7-5 lists some expenses to consider and provides an example of a three-day Boston to Dallas job trip. A targeted job campaign—visiting approximately twenty companies—can cost between $1,500 and $2,500, depending on the cities visited and the extent of your planning.

TABLE 7-5 General Expenses—Boston to Dallas Trip

Plane Fare (Super Saver)	$400	Filing Cabinet & System	
Car Rental (3 days)	$105	(used)	$ 30
Other Transportation and		Stationary	$ 25
Parking	$ 15	Résumé Printing	$ 20
Hotels (2 nights)	$ 80	Postage	$ 6
Meals	$ 60	Long-distance Phone Calls	$ 35

However, these initial costs should be evaluated in view of the potential increased earnings that could occur if the salary offer were higher from an out-of-town company—for example, $24,000 versus $19,000.

In spite of its obvious value, most MBAs will *not* use the suggested technique. For most, the targeted approach/travel plan cost will be regarded as an additional expense they just cannot afford. For a select few MBAs, the targeted approach/travel plan cost will be budgeted as a priority expense. They'll consider it no different from any other necessity such as food, shelter, tuition and books; it is the concluding expense of their MBA program.

The Campaign System

As is apparent in this entire book, you must be systematic and methodical throughout the job campaign. In particular, it is imperative you establish adequate record-keeping skills to monitor everything done and make the required follow-ups. The first essential part of this system is keeping a written list of prospects and copies of all correspondence. In future letters, it is important you cite the date and name of the individual contacted in previous correspondence. This helps avoid getting lost in the large corporation and its system. It is also important to determine the most appropriate size of each weekly mailing. The mailing must be a manageable one for you, given the other demands on your time. Make sure that your weekly mailings are not too large, so as to need more follow-up correspondence than you can handle. Similarly, however, you should avoid mailings that are too small—a subconscious way of prolonging the job campaign. While the mailings should be tailored to your own time dimensions, we have found that about twenty initial letters each week at regular weekly intervals is a good rule of thumb.

Keep a chart of the mailing date and follow-up letters dates for each company's correspondence. In cases where company interest develops, keep these communications in a separate company folder. And keep at least a brief copy of your files near the telephone. An executive may call unexpectedly a couple of days after receipt of your message and say, "Hello, this is Dave Smith returning your call." If you have many calls out, it may be difficult to relate "Dave Smith" to a specific company. With records close at hand, you should be able to quickly determine the company and avoid an embarrassing disorientation. Also, you'll have ready and accurate answers to questions about alternative dates and times. You see how important it is to have a really good system.

When appropriate, mention that several letters have been written to the company. Emphasize your desire to see some functional people in order to get a first-hand view of the job. At the same time, be sensitive to the executives' egos. Some personnel people may be offended by an MBA who does not acknowledge the personnel manager as the first hurdle toward further interviews.

Other Resources and Routes

Most MBAs approach prospective employers through various routes. Direct mail will be the path most frequently used. A few MBAs will make contact by telephone and follow up with a résumé, a technique requiring a certain level of confidence and good verbal skills. While most recent MBA graduates do not use employment agencies and executive recruiters, many MBAs with work experience do find these two agencies, described in later chapters, very beneficial. Referrals from faculty, previous employers, business friends, and family also provide a basis for successful contacts. You should use the channels suitable to your individual style and situation—almost anything that will help you reach your objective.

If you are still in the MBA program, the university you are attending keeps resources for your use. Although you should indeed undertake your own campaign, do not forget the MBA placement office. The placement office will have companies scheduled for interviewing and will also have contacts with many other companies. Establish a rapport with the placement office right away.

Other university groups and affiliates can also be very helpful. Get a list from the placement office of the MBA alumni living in the city of your choice, and enlist their help. Also seek out alumni who are working in industries and companies which interest you. University alumni clubs are often in major cities. They are important assets, so use them.

Newspaper advertisements can provide a limited number of opportunities for MBAs. Even though limited, investigate these ads, since they represent about 10 percent of the opportunities in the job market. Watch the newspaper in your desired city, particularly on Sundays. For example, the *Detroit Free Press* is a valuable source of job opportunities in the Detroit area. And other newspapers indicate job opportunities in more than the region. These papers include the Sunday *New York Times* and the *Wall Street Journal*. Besides indicating the jobs, these papers also can provide you with a sense of what is taking place in the overall executive job market.

When watching the newspaper ads, however, remember that responses to such advertisements are usually never read by top executives in the company; instead the responses are tightly screened, usually by the personnel department. Therefore, to ensure that your response is read, be very persuasive, and don't use too much fancy MBA jargon. Your cover letter should constantly refer to the enclosed résumé and should definitely ask for the interview. Then do something different to increase the possibility of an interview: on each of the five succeeding days send a copy of the letter and the résumé. This will help differentiate your response and indicate your earnestness and interest. Another way to differentiate your response is to send it certified mail.

In checking newspaper advertisements, do not fail to respond to a job opportunity because you don't meet the listed qualifications. While you need to meet most of the criteria, rarely do candidates have all of the qualifications. Good companies hire people, not credentials.

Be more careful in responding to newspaper advertisements with just box numbers and not company names, however if the description looks particularly exciting, follow it up. When the advertisement indicates both the company and a person to respond to, try the following: if the job is sponsored by a functional executive such as a plant manager, a vice-president of finance, or vice-president of planning, send the response directly to that individual by certified mail. Two days later, send a copy of the material to the appropriate personnel name indicated. This will help you reach the senior executive without offending the personnel department. Most senior executives like to be involved in the personnel selection—it is a nice change.

Some Summary Tips

1. Always package yourself in the strongest way possible. Make your campaign package dynamic, your marketing of yourself forceful.

2. A targeted job strategy will generally bring you better results faster than a hit-or-miss approach.

3. Good managerial jobs are rarely publicized; you have to find them. Search for your opportunities.

4. Never forget that there are more goods jobs around than there are MBAs to fill them.

5. If you impress a company with your perception and ability to think, frequently a position will be found for you.

6. Ask MBA graduates from previous years how they found their jobs.

7. Use fellow MBAs as support during your campaign. Each has similar problems; be sure to swap job leads. This is the time to help each other, not compete.

8. Each target market in the country has different characteristics. You have to become familiar with the one you are interested in.

9. Determine how much time you have after graduation before having a job becomes mandatory. This is particularly important if your search is centered in a distant city.

10. If you plan to work in another city, make at least one visit to that city. However, you can utilize your home as a base city while mapping your distant job campaign.

11. Make as many contacts as possible. While in all job searches a referral is crucial, in a new city it is a must.

Meet bankers, people in education, physicians, real estate professionals, insurance and general business people to provide you with many introductions in a new city.

12. Utilize university services: your business school librarian and the business books in the library, placement services, periodicals and newspapers.

13. Always try to identify the company executive who has the power to hire you and who has the problem to be solved.

14. During your search, get help from a wide variety of people, not just your immediate type.

8

Interviewing Strategies

The preceding chapters—and all your work to date—have led you to this point: the interview. If you have carefully set your goals, prepared your materials, and contacted the right employers, you will be able to look forward to and actually enjoy the interviews. In this chapter, we'll give you some tips on what to expect next and how to be ready.

Setting the Stage

Once you have obtained the interview, it is up to you to sell yourself. One important aspect of this is to study the company and its personnel well in advance of the actual interview. This does not entail merely stopping by the library or the career center the morning of your interview to read company literature, or casually asking professors or other individuals if they know anything about the company. Thorough interview preparation means a great deal of time and hard work, but if you want the job with that particular company, it is well worth the effort. In fact, it is necessary in today's competitive job market.

Start by researching the industry as a whole. You should

have already done some of this research when you were deciding what to do and where to do it. Analyze the industry carefully now, particularly past and current trends, and then study the specifics of the company that wants to interview you. Look at its major competition and the primary opportunities and threats facing it. Determine why you are interested in that company.

We've already mentioned several sources of information on companies and industries. One other valuable source for consumer goods companies is Advertising Age's *100 Leading Advertisers*, published during August of each year. This issue presents information on sales results, advertising expenditures, market strategy, new products, company product lines, company organization and executive personnel. Other industries and companies also have information of this type.

Another valuable reference is the *Value Line Report* on each company. This newsletter provides a ten-year summary of key financial statistics that can be used to develop possible questions for the interviewer. Also, the *Value Line* capsulizes key trends in the business and succinctly describes the operations by product lines.

Perhaps the most useful reference is the company's own annual report. For these, you would have to have sent post cards requesting the reports months before beginning your job campaign, thereby ensuring you'd have them in time for the interview. For other sources of information, see Chapter 4.

You may be interviewing ten to twenty companies on an initial basis, so you need a significant amount of preparation. Your research material must be extremely well organized for instant use. At this point you should break up your general files and start a separate folder for each target company with all the information about that specific company, including recent articles you might have collected during the previous six months. Also use this folder to keep copies of your correspondence. Study the information so you know it well.

Early Considerations

Although your references should be readily accessible so you may review a company quickly and efficiently, the initial interview seldom allows time for long discussions about the company. The most important discussion in the initial interview is about *you* and how your background, accomplishments, talents, and interests make you a viable candidate for the position. The essential research at this point, then, will be to know the following about each company:

1. Organizational structure. What are the divisions? Which are the largest? How has the company diversified?

2. Its products. What are *key* products—the ones for which the company is famous? What product lines are *growing*? What *new* products have been introduced?

3. Its sales growth. How much did the company grow last year? In what areas? Are any trends apparent?

4. Its profits. How much did profits increase or decrease last year? What is the company's financial picture and outlook in the short and long run?

5. Its structure. What *type* of product management system exists at the company? Is it highly structured and sophisticated or much less so?

This information will give you the basis for carefully answering the question almost always asked: Why does our company interest you? For example, an MBA was recently asked: "Why are you talking to our company about a product management job?"

"Well, Mr. _____, my career objective is to reach a senior management position through a career path in product management. Your company is a leader in consumer marketing and you have a product management system which is less structured than some of the other packaged goods companies. This means I can take on more responsibility early on and therefore make a contribution to the company in a much shorter time. For this reason, I am very interested in your company."

Usually this type of short answer is sufficient in an initial interview. If the interviewer probes more deeply, you should be ready with some specific facts, such as last year's percentage sales increase, increases (and by how much) in the advertising expenditures last year, or that the recent new product campaign was impressive in terms of sales or profits achieved.

Preparation: You

A word of caution: Don't ever prepare your research on the company to the detriment of your personal preparation. Just as the résumé development is a creative process, so is interviewing. Many call it a game or an audition, but whatever your view, there is a great deal of personal preparation as well. Competition among MBAs is keen, and preparation will keep your mistakes to a minimum.

Constantly think of the way you're positioning yourself to the company. The first step is always to understand the needs of the company. For most management spots, this entails high analytical ability, good written and verbal communication skills, initiative, leadership, and maturity. How can you show that you have these qualities? This is your objective when you attempt to position yourself in the job market. The interviewer must make a "go or no go" decision in usually a thirty minute initial interview period. In that brief time, he or she can only obtain a feeling about you, and that person's intuition will be based a great deal on your personality, poise, maturity, appearance, and ability to verbalize. You must practice and develop succinct, clear, intelligent responses to commonly asked questions.

Personality significantly influences whether or not a rapport is established between you and the interviewer. While a very experienced interviewer can eliminate any likes and dislikes of an applicant, many companies have hired people who interview very well and do very poorly on the job. If the interviewer tries to rattle you, do not lose your composure. If necessary, stall until you can collect your thoughts. Your personality is an asset. If it is warm and friendly, use it to the fullest extent. If your personality is not a strong point, work on it; perhaps some counseling will help. Do not think that it doesn't matter—it does. All business today is based on interpersonal relationships.

Always practice the way in which you will answer the questions. Some MBAs use audiovisual equipment to practice; this helps identify distracting mannerisms, poor posture, or poor eye contact. Remember—much of what you say is evaluated in terms of how quickly you think on your feet, how well you can organize your thoughts, and how clearly you speak. Practice will help build confidence and allow you to relax during the actual interviews.

One of the most important reasons for a bad first impression is lack of interview practice. If you are overly concerned about interviews, be sure to get some training in interview techniques. And practice.

Some Typical Questions

The following are some specific questions that are asked in the majority of MBA interviews.

"Why did you go to your particular school?" If you went to one of the top fifteen or twenty MBA schools, this question will be easy to answer. Even having attended one of these, you had better have some specific reasons why. If you went to a lesser-known school, which will be the case with most MBAs, you should be able to answer why you selected the one you did. Was this the only school where you were accepted? What criteria did you use in the decision? It is almost always the best policy to accentuate the positive in your response to this question. Do not indicate that it was a toss-of-the-coin decision. Make a positive answer such as the following: "My school (by name) is an excellent school with a growing reputation. It offered the kind of curriculum I wanted (mention any special things) and also has a reputation for good faculty, especially in my area of concentration (by name)." Since there is no correct answer for this question, there is no way to really win or lose. Be positive.

"Why do you want a job in the particular field you specialized in (such as product management, financial management, sales or advertising management)?" You might indicate that the position would allow you to use both your analytical and interpersonal skills. You should also mention that the position is exciting to you and you believe it is fast-paced. Your general response should be specifically tied into items on your résumé, such as past jobs (where you developed your interpersonal skills), or business-school-sponsored consulting projects (that dealt with specific subject matter), or your success as a manager. For your management decision-making simulation group, the possibilities are endless. Of course, the more you know about the position and the more you practice, the better your answers will be.

Other questions are likely to be:

1. What are your strengths?

2. What are your weaknesses?

3. What is your biggest accomplishment in life?

4. What are two other of your outstanding accomplishments?

5. What does a position in the specific area mean to you?

6. What does it take to be a good manager? Show me examples in your background where you displayed these qualities.

7. What was your first job? Earnings? Your second, third, etc.?

8. What was your favorite marketing, financial management, or production case?

9. What do you personally want from a company?

10. What other companies are of interest to you?

11. What is your philosophy on governmental regulations?

12. How did you prepare for this interview?

13. What are your goals?

14. What is your best trait?

15. Describe the MBA program at your school.

16. What other types of positions are you pursuing?

17. Describe your strategy to get a specific position.

18. What was your favorite course at graduate school?

19. What was your least favorite course?

20. What is the *main* reason that you would make a good manager?

21. Why did you decide to go to college?

22. Why did you choose an undergraduate major?

23. What criteria are you using to evaluate and choose a company?

24. What mistakes did you make in your most important job?

25. Why did you get an MBA?

26. Did your school prepare you well in your area of concentration? Explain.

27. What are some adjectives that describe you?

28. What is the hardest decision you've ever made?

29. What was your boss good at in your most important job?

30. What was your boss's biggest weakness?

31. What are your short-range objectives? Your long-range objectives?

32. What are you looking for in a job?

33. How long will you stay with us?

34. What new goals have you developed during your MBA experience?

35. What do you expect to be doing five years from today?

36. What is your definition of success?

37. Do you feel you will prosper better in a large or small company?

38. Why do you want to work for us?

39. Given a choice, which company would you work for, at which job, and for what salary?

40. Why should we hire you?

41. How long do you think it would be before you will make a contribution to this company?

42. How would you evaluate companies you worked for?

43. What features of previous jobs have you disliked?

44. How do you handle criticism?

45. How do you feel about working for a woman? A man? A minority?

46. How do you work under pressure and deadlines?

47. What salary do you think you are worth?

48. Would you go through an MBA program if you were starting out again?

49. Would you be out to get your boss's job?

50. What makes you feel you have top-management potential?

51. Tell me all about yourself.

52. What was the last nonbusiness book you read? The last movie you saw? And the last sporting event you attended?

53. What is your philosophy of management?

54. Do you like line or staff positions? Why?

55. Have you ever fired anyone? Why? How did you feel about it?

56. Have you ever hired anyone? What do you look for when hiring someone?

57. Are you creative? Give me an example of your creativity.

58. Are you a leader? Illustrate your leadership capabilities.

59. What job options do you have currently? With whom? Describe each situation.

60. Are you interested in any causes? Which ones?

61. How do business conditions appear to you over the next several years?

62. What do you think of the present investment climate?

63. What do you think of the government's economic program? Why?

64. What do you think of labor unions? Have you ever dealt with one?

65. Which do you prefer working with, figures or words?

66. Would you prefer doing a job, developing a job, or managing others who are doing the job?

67. How do you feel about job-related travel?

68. Are you willing to relocate?

69. If you were me what type of person would you seek for this job?

70. What questions do you have for me?

71. If we don't hire you where would you like to work?

72. What major problems have you overcome and how did you do it?

In addition to these more personal and job-related questions, you will probably be asked some questions about your area of concentration. This will be especially the case if you are being interviewed by a line executive of a particular functional area.

Besides reviewing the preceding questions, be prepared to answer all possible *whys* concerning your background. Everything you ever did could be questioned. WHY? WHY? WHY? Again, you must tailor these answers to show that you have the desired qualities for a management position and that you have established and achieved objectives.

In selling yourself through your answers, do not stress experience when speaking about past jobs, but rather accomplishments. Employers want an MBA who is on the fast track in life. Just having work experience is not enough. What did you accomplish? Did you get promoted before more experienced workers? Were you given responsibility in a short time? Having four years of full-time work experience where you did not steadily advance to higher levels of salary and responsibility can often do more harm than good. The interviewer can easily get the impression that you got your MBA because you couldn't get anywhere without it. This is not the fast-track highly talented, highly capable person they are seeking. Therefore be careful about your experiences and try to emphasize the accomplishments in these past jobs.

Know Your Résumé

It has been indicated throughout this book that your résumé outlines your qualifications and your accomplishments. Since your résumé is the best possible description of your assets, use it as a basis for what you tell a prospective employer. Know your résumé thoroughly and develop the capability to remember every facet of it. Each sentence should be a jumping off spot to selling yourself.

Prepare for your interview as you would a speech to be delivered without notes, being careful not to make it so automatic that it sounds like a recording. Learn how to talk about yourself without any inhibitions, emphasizing your most important talents. Be able to converse fluently, know what you are talking about, and have confidence in being able to handle questions; that may well be the deciding factor for a prospective employer. All of this preparation will help eliminate nervousness and allow you to project yourself as a capable manager.

The interviewer will expect you to clearly describe your background, accomplishments and interests. For example, if you are looking for involvement in product management, you'll be expected to know something about market research, pricing, advertising management, and distribution channels. As an operations manager, you'll be expected to know something about costs, plant management, piecework rates, labor relations, and computer-aided production machinery. As someone interested in finance you'll want to know something about various accounting procedures, financial statements, investment practices, and certainly computer management skills. However, the interviewer will probably not be looking for knowledge of details in this functional area but rather for your ability to conceptualize.

Fear Avoidance

While most MBAs have the correct attitude during the interview, they very frequently are afraid of failure. They have all the intellect, drive, common sense, and managerial potential to be invited to join their favorite company, but somehow that invitation never comes. A fear of failure gets in their way and causes a bad interview to occur.

Indeed, shyness itself is a form of fear. It can be caused by a physical problem or an imagined failing. You can help overcome shyness by reflecting on your major assets and strengths. Try not to be overwhelmed by interviewers who, by reason of reputation, wealth, education and managerial position, seem awesome. Remember that there are no supermen or superwomen in this world. Most of us are good at some things, and all of us can learn.

You can help control fear in interviews by doing some of the following:

- Try to determine reasons for your fears. Think carefully about your assets and your problems.

- Know your strengths and weaknesses completely, so that you can use them to sell yourself. Practice doing this with a friend or with a video tape recorder.

- Be confident in your dress and grooming.

- If you cannot overcome nervousness, enter into as many interview situations as possible for practice. Remember that first interviews are often unsuccessful. Gradually your nervousness will disappear. Remember, of course, that a certain degree of nervousness is to be expected in any pressure situation.

As you answer questions about yourself, be affirmative in describing your qualifications and accomplishments. It is most important to be forceful. As in business, it is always important to be decisive; never appear to be unsure of yourself. Have good answers to the following questions about yourself:

1. What do you do best?

2. What do you like to do?

3. What things would you rather stay away from?

4. What are your goals in life?

5. What have you missed doing?

6. What are your greatest strengths?

7. What are your greatest weaknesses?

In order to minimize before-interview apprehension, concentrate on your best qualities for the few minutes prior to the interview. Recall a situation in which you have been confident, enthusiastic, and professional. Be prepared to be yourself. Be natural, relaxed, positive, and friendly. Refresh your memory on what general qualities employers are looking for in potential management talent: maturity, drive, communication skills, intelligence, common sense, knowledge, and the ability to deal with people.

Types of Interviews

What types of interviews are you likely to encounter? Keep in mind that many interviewers are not very good at interviewing. Interviewing is not a part of their daily routine, and they are frequently ill at ease and often not knowledgeable about all the specifics of the business. Usually when you interview with a seasoned top executive, that person will put you totally at ease.

Some interviewers are nasty. They belittle you, assume a superior attitude, and generally try to undermine your self-confidence. This type of interviewer, when challenged on some statements, is likely to retreat. You will also encounter some nervous people. Just stay calm and be patient, and do not let anyone abuse you. No job is worth allowing yourself to be treated poorly. Besides, you do not want to work for a company that interviews that way.

You will encounter interviewers who show no interest in you and appear bored. Some may even be jealous of you.

You will encounter interviewers who do all the talking. In these instances, try tactfully to present your story before you leave. If your interviewer allows himself or herself to be interrupted on the telephone, just keep repeating your story until you get it across.

Some interviewers are very interested in you and listen to everything you say. As a result, you can talk too much, revealing things which you should not. Be very careful with this type of interview; balance is important.

While some interviewers take copious notes, this really is not necessary since they already have your résumé. Try to have this interviewer look at you as you ask and answer questions. You can change or help control the interview by asking questions about the interviewer's job, the company, the people you might be working for, or anything else pertinent to your visit.

The Actual Interview

Regardless of the extent of your other preparation, the interview is critical. There is no need to control the interview; a good interview is an exchange of ideas between the interviewer and you. The interviewer controls his or her portion of the interview with questions, and you control your part by your answers, your sales presentation, and by your questions. You will be in control as long as you know what you are talking about and can communicate this knowledge properly.

How an interview begins depends for the most part on how it was established. Is it an interview on campus? Was it a result of your mailing a résumé, a sales or broadcast letter, a referral, an arrangement by an executive search firm, or an answer to an advertisement? Try to make the atmosphere of the interview relaxed by letting the interviewer do most of the talking. Good interviewers will simultaneously try to put you at ease.

Be careful about using humor. Many interviewers find the injection of humor into a business conversation offensive. In addition, you never know how a stranger is going to react to your humor. What some consider funny is anathema to others.

Be honest in your answers about yourself. If there are some skeletons in your closet about why you left a previous job, be factual but throw everything possible into a positive light. Try to indicate how you have learned from your experiences as well as from your education. While having an imperfect scorecard in life is nothing to be ashamed of, not learning from a situation is counterproductive. Never be negative about previous employers or bosses; no one is simpatico with everyone. Keep everything you say practical, not euphoric, but above all positive.

Since you have obtained your MBA degree, you should know the difference between line and staff positions. Staff jobs support; line jobs execute. While staff jobs can teach you a great deal about a company, ultimately, if you want power and position, you want line responsibility.

Frequently you will be asked about long-term objectives. You could respond by indicating that you wish to develop your capabilities; that you wish to become very knowledgeable in your current area of specialization; that you wish to contribute in a maximum way to profitability; that you wish to be instrumental in developing young executives; and that you are looking for growth toward becoming a senior member of management.

Sometimes you will be asked where you expect to be five years hence. You should indicate you are looking forward to growth and to a better job. You should expect to have a job commensurate with an ability that contributes to the goals of the company. You should always want to be learning as well as contributing.

Always be prepared to talk about the last book you read, the last play or movie you saw, which newspapers and magazines you read, or the last lecture you attended. Progressive businesses want broad-gauged executives. Narrow people generally make poor managers.

From your end, you will be looking for personal fulfillment as well as the opportunity to be an effective manager. Try to project the impression that you are stable and look forward to a career which will last as long as you can learn and grow and can assume increasing degrees of responsibility.

Many interviewers will ask why you want to work for their company. Your research should give you the answer to this question, and certainly the company's reputation, location, growth history, and opportunities provide additional reasons.

You will be asked by many interviewers, "Why should we hire you?" In response, don't be negative about competition, particularly if you are not sure who it is. Once again stress yourself and your accomplishments. Make everything totally positive. Always talk about your success stories. If you refer to some of the negative areas, do so only in the context of the learning process.

You may be asked what you learned in your MBA program. This is an excellent question to answer, as it allows you to show that you are a learner. Willingness and the desire to learn will probably be important elements in any company's evaluation process.

Some interviewers may ask you to evaluate a company with which you have been previously associated. In response to this question, always say something positive before making such general negative comments as it was too small, it was too large, it was too structured, it was too slow in growth, or it did not have enough new products or it was losing out competitively. Never divulge confidential information or speak pejoratively about a previous employer. If you do find this is necessary, at least project the image of having been assertive and decisive. Always use the examples of work that put you in the best possible light.

Never indicate any problems about working for a woman, a man, or a member of a minority. If you do have such bias, try to understand it. Get some help if necessary so that you can learn to cope with the situation.

Many interviewers will ask you if you can work under pressure. Describe a situation when this was true and how you handled it. By the same token, a seasoned executive who does not know how to handle a situation admits it and seeks time to find a solution.

A favorite interview question is, "What is your biggest weakness?" Perhaps you are impatient. Perhaps you are stubborn. Perhaps you will not compromise and you are not diplomatic. All of these so-called weaknesses can be re-positioned as strengths.

Many interviewers ask, "Are you the type who will be after the boss's job?" The answer—of course—is yes, given the hope that the boss is going to move up. You always want to be working for a person who is moving to a higher-level management position.

You may be asked, "In jobs where you have done some supervising, what have your subordinates thought of you?" The answer should always be, "They have respected me."

Suppose someone asks you about your philosophy of management. It is hoped you believe in efficiency and creativity; have an understanding of how the changing environment affects your business; believe in fairness to stockholders and employers; use management by objective and by exception; believe in the profit motive and ethical standards; and have the ability to withstand the typical and not-so-typical business problems.

What would you say if asked how you would feel about firing a subordinate? Being a fair as well as competent manager, you would of course have previously given this employer several evaluations. You would let that employee know how he or she was doing— what was proceeding properly and what was proceeding improperly. As a good manager you will have operated so constructively and openly with all subordinates that if it becomes necessary to discharge or demote someone, it will not be a surprise.

What about your experience in hiring people? In hiring, a manager looks to fill the needs of the job, seeks someone with long-term potential, and wants someone who understands the profit responsibility and has the ability to train subordinates.

You will probably be asked some questions about budgets. As an MBA, if you have not supervised a budget yourself, you certainly have studied the process in the classroom. Therefore be prepared to discuss one or two real-life situations and your own philosophy of budgeting.

Questions You Should Ask

In almost every case, the interviewer will ask you if there are any questions that he or she can answer. This usually occurs at the end of the interview. It is a critical period. You should have intelligent, incisive questions prepared that will indicate you understand the subtleties of your field and the company in particular. Even if you already know the answer to the question, ask it if it's a good question. For example, you could ask what the company's criteria are for investment analysis or what's the single most important quality looked for in selecting managers. Other possible questions are:

1. What criteria did you use to choose this company?

2. Why did you choose market research?

3. What's the negative side of public accounting?

4. Are you satisfied with the career opportunities at the company?

5. What are the weaknesses of your company?

6.   When and how are new managers evaluated?

7.   How does operations management turnover at your company compare to most of the other companies in your industry?

8.   What fields will your company be growing in, during the next ten years?

9.   What is the hardest part of your job as a member of top management with this company?

10.   How does your company differ from the other packaged goods firms in terms of the product management system?

11.   What is the most important ability necessary for success in corporate accounting?

At this point, your previous research will be very helpful. Perhaps the company has been losing market share in a certain product category. Ask why, and ask what defense is being planned.

Most interviewers appreciate it if you are interested enough in the company to so indicate. Some people feel it is better not to seem too interested in a particular company, and this strategy may work for some candidates, but it is usually not the best one for most MBAs. This is particularly the case if the interview came about as a result of your aggressiveness and initiative. In this situation, it makes little sense to play hard to get.

It should be stressed again that the *initial* interview is short. You must be sensitive to the time constraint and avoid continuing that interview when the interviewer wants it to end. Therefore, usually only one or two good questions can be asked. However, one exception to this general rule occurred when an interviewer began the interview with the statement, "I'm not going to ask you about your background or résumé. You ask me questions, and I'll find out what I need to know by the questions you ask." Needless to say, a lot of questions were required to fill the 45-minute period.

You should be enthusiastic about your area of interest. You should also indicate that you like what you've read about the company and look forward to talking with some other members of the company about mutual employment objectives. Remember, it is a two-way street, and you should be as anxious to make a personality fit as the company is. This of course can only be done through a day-long second interview, and such second interviews are granted about 20 percent of the time. In most cases, be enthusiastic about being invited back and say so!

Recording Impressions

After each interview, take some time to carefully evaluate the session. Keep a record of the difficult questions so you can develop better responses for future interviews. Note questions that weren't asked for possible inclusion in the follow-up letter. And those areas in which you gave a poor response should be researched and also mentioned in the follow-up letter. Also record your good responses. After a few interviews, you'll develop a sense of when an interviewer was impressed or unimpressed.

A useful device is a simple chart listing each company interviewed; the date, name, and title of the interviewer(s); place of interview; position; and the "next step." This chart should also include a rating of how the interview went and what you feel your chance is of being invited for a second interview. The process helps sharpen your judgment and your perceptions as you see how accurate your predictions are.

Use the chart to discuss your entire job strategy with counselors and faculty advisors. It also allows an advisor to have an overall view of your strategy, should you need to reassess it. Be leery of interviewers who are extremely nice, and who tell you that you are a good prospect and how they wished there were something available. These easy interviews often do not lead anywhere, particularly when they are with the Personnel Department.

Follow-Up Letters

For the well-organized MBA, there is no excuse for *not* sending a brief follow-up letter after an initial interview. Often the final decision as to who is invited back is not made for several weeks. This gives the company time to interview dozens of candidates at different schools, looking for the "stars." For example, General Foods usually interviews over eighty MBAs from the Harvard Business School alone. Some companies even wait until their total recruiting is completed before making decisions on whom to bring back.

For these reasons, a follow-up letter is very important. It can be successfully used to thank the interviewer for the opportunity to interview; reaffirm your interest in a managerial opportunity with the company; ask any questions that were not covered in the interview; and offer to supply any additional information, such as references or transcripts. Follow-up letters can be even briefer if time is short, but they definitely should be sent. This personal touch favorably impresses an interviewer and may be a big help in getting that second interview and, ultimately, hearing that job offer.

Getting Invited Back

Getting invited back for a second interview is a natural consequence of the variables described in this book. The odds will certainly vary from candidate to candidate, depending basically on how good he or she is and how well he or she conducted the job campaign, but if you've paid attention and done your homework, it should happen for you.

Companies differ in their methodology. A larger recruiter such as General Foods will usually notify a candidate within a week of the initial interview, set up a date within the next few weeks, and notify him or her of the results within two weeks of the second interview. On the other hand, some companies do not even know how many candidates will be needed until March or April. These companies might wait until all the college recruiting is finished before deciding on which candidates to bring to company headquarters.

Some companies use both approaches concurrently. This occurs when an MBA receives a letter soon after the first interview indicating that the company was impressed and will be in contact again several months later regarding the second interview. Sometimes this means that the MBA has been placed in an intermediary status—a good MBA prospect but not a star. For some candidates, a few last-minute telephone calls were received in late April from some of these companies after other offers had already been accepted with more decisive companies. The companies either misjudged their needs or failed to get as many star candidates to accept their offer as they anticipated. Therefore, a small second job market for MBAs opens up in late April; this can provide some alternatives for MBAs still seeking management positions.

The second interview is even more demanding than the first. You usually make the travel arrangements, with all expenses paid by the company; you usually *initially* pay for all expenses except a hotel, which the company usually reserves and charges directly to its account. You are reimbursed quickly, often the same day as the interview. However, some companies will provide an expense form and return envelope; this means a one- or two-week delay in receipt of payment. Whichever the case, you'll find extra cash and credit cards extremely useful, since you could easily travel to five different cities in a two-week period.

Many companies assign an MBA graduate of a previous year the task of taking you to dinner the night before the second interview. This is almost *always* nonevaluative, and it gives you a chance to ask questions about the first year's training and procedures. Some companies will provide an itinerary in advance, often with a brief biographical sketch of the executives with whom you'll be speaking. (Obviously, you have researched the company and its product lines before the interview.) Your dinner companion can often provide some insights into the people you will be meeting the following day, such as "he or she loves sailing," or "he hates unions." Remember, often the best interviews result when the interviewer realizes he or she has a common interest with you; usually this is a hobby. Such prior knowledge gleaned from your host can help you position yourself a little better.

There will be anywhere from three to eight interviews during your second visit to the company. Some of these are the people for whom you would actually be working. If you are interested in a marketing position, you will probably interview with a marketing manager, several group product managers, and some product managers, plus be taken to lunch by an assistant. Your basic strategy should be similar to that used for the initial interview, since these are merely a number of 45-minute interviews all in one day. Therefore, the same preparation, questions, and practice recommended for the initial interview section should be followed.

Often, the interviewers are assigned different roles during this session. For example, one interviewer may explore your childhood to a great extent. This interviewer will ask you what you were like as a child, in what areas you were outstanding, what people remember you for, and what your brothers and sisters did. Another interviewer might conduct the "stress" interview during which his basically hostile line of questioning is designed to unnerve you. Perhaps the marketing manager will spend his or her time telling you how great the company is. Be prepared for anything, and then you will have no problems. Usually, most interviews are pleasant and easy going. In fact, there seems to be a correlation between a company's having a management system and conducting tough interviews. The less-structured companies often show their informality by being informal in these second interviews. One manager emphasized this point by putting his feet on the desk during the interview and assuming such a relaxed profile that the MBA thought the interview was about to be terminated.

Again, detailed knowledge about the company is of secondary importance in these interviews. The main focus is still on *you*, and each interviewer wants to understand as much about you as possible during the allotted time. An interviewer will often ask you to hold off questions until the last five or ten minutes so that this objective can be accomplished. Again, direct the conversation toward your strengths and knowledge whenever possible, assuming you are thoroughly prepared. Since many of the interviewers will not have a great deal of knowledge about your particular MBA program, this is an excellent opportunity to prove yourself and the worth of your education. One candidate received an offer from a company largely because of an outstanding answer to the question, "How do you set up a marketing research project?" The interviewer was so impressed with the candidate's superior marketing knowledge and commitment that he moved ahead of some fairly sharp competitors.

Some MBAs bring copies of various consulting reports or class projects. Usually, these will be only quickly glanced at by the interviewer, although some executives find these exhibits interesting, and they can be used to fill a lull in the conversation. Be careful, however, about forcing these exhibits on the interviewer; the interviewer can tell if you are attempting to get out of talking. If exhibits are used, they should only be referred to and then left on the desk or table. The interviewer will then have the option to examine the material or not.

What Companies Seek

When engaged in the interviewing process, always assess what the company is seeking. The primary criterion of the company is likely to be ability—usually analytical ability and then interpersonal skills. Of course, the company will want to be sure you can work under pressure, that you communicate well, and that you are a self-starter, a leader, an innovative hard-worker and creative person. Companies are usually interested in a fast-track type who is very bright and has no trouble getting things accomplished. Be sure you present that image in the interview.

Intelligence and initiative are probably the two most important traits companies value. They assume that most MBAs are intelligent. A well-thought-out job campaign will support an MBA's claims to having initiative. Whenever possible, indicate through an actual experience or accomplishment some of these desired traits.

Companies are risk-averse just as consumers are. A company likes to know that you are a top candidate and that other companies want you too. You need to act like a top candidate and evaluate the company as a top candidate would. Ask some tough questions. Why you should join the company? What are the company's advantages over some of its competitors? Use the knowledge from your MBA business policy course to determine if the company is integrative, diversifying, growing, or stagnating. Determine if there are opportunities for a fast-track MBA like yourself who is willing to work hard to get ahead. This will indicate that you are a selective candidate who is making a logical, intelligent, informed career choice. Obviously your evaluation procedure should only be introduced if and when the interviewer asks if you have any questions or when you are asked to explain your criteria in selecting a company. The evaluation procedure then becomes a natural part of the interview process, not something you've forced into the situation.

What You Seek

The choice of a job is as much yours as it is the company's. It is therefore very important to develop your own job criteria—indeed, it is expected of top MBA candidates. Business decisions, as well as personal ones, are guided by criteria. And since you'll be expected to defend your decisions once you're with the company, you should also be doing it now as you evaluate job situations. This will allow both you and the company to match your criteria.

The criteria can be sharpened by listening. Your questions should be about the company, how it is different from others, and why you chose it. The important element is the personality fit between you and the company. How comfortable do you feel with these people? Are your personal interests and hobbies similar? These criteria will be extremely helpful in deciding which job offer to accept later; more about that in Chapter 11.

We are reminded of one MBA applicant who applied to

M.I.T.'s Sloan School Program and the Harvard Business School and was refused admission by both. One of the universities indicated in a postmortem interview that they felt that his applying to two such vastly different programs meant that he did not know what he wanted. A similar situation could occur in the job campaign. Therefore you should establish criteria somewhat in light of the company's expectations. For example, if you are a marketing candidate with Procter and Gamble, your reasons for wanting that job could be that it is the top marketing company in the world and you wish to learn from experts. While at Nestle's Company, your reasons might be that you want a less-structured product management system—professional, yet informal; a company with strong international orientation; and a company with a reputation for high-quality products you can believe in. In fact, a good question to ask the interviewer is what his or her criteria were—why he or she chose to work for the company and why he or she likes it.

Usually during the initial interview you will not be certain of all the reasons for your choice of a company and position. It will not be until the longer second interviews that you can get a real feeling for the atmosphere and personality of a company, factors which ultimately become the decision variables for both the company and the MBA candidate.

Some Summary Tips

1. Dress appropriately for your interviews. The correct wardrobe will help you feel good about yourself.

2. Research each company before going to the interview.

3. Don't try so hard to please the interviewer that you get uptight yourself. Put your own feelings first; feel good about yourself.

4. Don't try to control the interview; control your responses.

5. Don't take notes during the interview unless absolutely necessary.

6. Smoke only if your interviewer does. Offer a firm

handshake upon meeting and leaving your inter-viewer.

7. Maintain eye contact with the interviewer throughout the session.

8. If your interviewer invites you to use first names, do so. This is more prevalent in the Midwest and West.

9. Don't be a never-ending talker. Do not be hostile or overly aggressive. Do state your convictions diplo-matically.

10. Listen to what the interviewer says. Refer to his or her comments when assembling your answers to ques-tions.

11. Use the answers to questions to sell yourself. Ask open-ended questions in response to the interviewer who talks in broad concepts.

12. Be honest and open, but don't confess your weak-nesses and liabilities.

13. Send a thank-you note.

9

Employment Agencies— for the MBA?

Many MBAs are in a quandary concerning employment agencies. What are they? Are they of value in obtaining the best job? How much do their services cost? In order to put an employment agency to optimal use, you must understand the nature of this business, the basic types, when to use an agency, and how to choose one.

What Employment Agencies Are

An employment agency is a body broker filling the gap between employer needs and available personnel. If a company has a need for an MBA with a strong marketing and statistics background and with some project experience, the employer sends a note to the agency describing the position and its requirements. The agency then selects qualified people from its files to be candidates for that position The candidates would have been screened previously by agency personnel and their names held until a suitable vacancy came along. From the list of candidates the employer receives, the interviews are arranged. Once a candidate is selected, in most cases the company pays the agency a fee, the amount dependent upon the position and its corresponding salary.

Most agency placements for MBA-level positions occur as described above, although some agencies charge a fee to the individual, but this kind of agency usually deals with job classifications that are not commensurate with MBA-level positions. If an employment agency indicates that you will have to pay a fee, it probably won't have the kind of job you want.

What are the types of agencies and how do they work? Since it requires little capital to start an employment agency, there are many start-ups and failures each year. Basically, anyone who has some knowledge in the personnel field can open an employment agency, except in those states where licensing is required. Many successful agencies have been started by an executive in the personnel area who left a corporate position to begin his or her own enterprise.

With the only requirements being some contacts, a telephone, stationery, and business cards it is no wonder the turnover rate in employment agencies is so high. Yet with new agencies constantly being established, there has been little net change in the total number existing in the United States. These agencies can be broken down into categories based on the major type of personnel handled: in other words, secretarial, domestic, and engineering.

In respect to MBA-level positions, agencies can be categorized on either a functional or an industrial level. On a functional basis there exist agencies that specialize in accounting and financial personnel, sales and marketing personnel, or EDP and systems personnel. Other agencies specialize in various managerial levels in certain types of industry—for example, computer, advertising, metals, or insurance. Only certain agencies handle MBA-level positions, making it necessary to carefully screen agencies before choosing one.

Some agencies have established branch offices or partnerships in other cities. For example, Romac Associates, specializing in EDP and financial personnel, has offices in various cities on the East Coast. Each partner in an office is autonomous, yet contributes to the entire corporate placement effort through financial contribution as well as by supplying information on positions and personnel to the system. In this way a person indicating an interest in Boston, for example, can be expediently matched with an opening in Raleigh.

Other employment agencies join one of two nationwide networks: the National Association of Personnel Consultants (NAPC) and the National Personnel Associates (NPA). The National Association of

Personnel Consultants, previously called the National Employment Association, is a trade association which any employment agency can join. National Personnel Associates is a cooperative of agencies who share placement; it has restricted membership. The network of agencies provides the means by which both the applicant and employer receive nationwide exposure, thus wider opportunities exist for matching employees with employers. You can obtain free directories of the affiliates in a given area by writing to either of the associations. Their addresses are given on page 143.

Agency Operations

While the operations of an agency vary, depending on its nature and size, generally the following procedure occurs. A company submits a description of the job opening and the qualifications needed. The company has selected the agency it feels is best suited to find the most qualified candidates for that position and most companies have established solid working relationships with an agency through previous dealings. The job description will be as detailed as possible indicating any personality traits and characteristics relating to success in the position. Where possible, the company will rank the qualifications and requirements in order of importance. In addition, they indicate the salary range and timetable for employment. A quality agency treats all such company information confidentially.

The agency searches its files for all candidates that fit the requirements. For those agencies tied into a national network, this includes querying all member agencies for candidates in their area. If no candidates are available, most agencies will place an advertisement in a newspaper or trade journal describing the job and its qualifications. The cost of this advertisement is usually borne by the agency but in some cases the company takes care of the ad expenses.

Résumés of qualified candidates are sent to the company. Depending on the relationship the agency has with the employers, it does at least a minimum amount of pre-screening. This screening sometimes is very extensive, so that only the résumé of the three or four best candidates are sent to the company.

It is important to understand the agency operations from the MBA's perspective. The first aspect is the agency's determination that it can be helpful in placing a candidate. This decision is usually based on an initial telephone conversation, followed by a review of the MBA's résumé, and finally an interview either by telephone or in person. Whenever possible, conduct a personal interview; personal interviews usually get results. During this interview you can get a chance to assess the agency and to inform the interviewer of personal notes of interests, skills, and capabilities. In addition, you form a personal bond between yourself and agency personnel. At this time you'll also be queried regarding any special experience or education so the agency may establish your "selling points." If the agency feels that your qualifications and interests are in line with its job opportunities, you are given an application blank. The application forms vary from agency to agency.

Then one of two things happen. If the agency knows of any job opportunities that match your capabilities, salary requirements, and interests, the company is immediately contacted. If there are no immediate job opportunities, then your application is placed on file to be pulled when an appropriate opportunity arises.

When an opportunity arises and you are invited to the company for an interview, the agency usually prepares you with a briefing. The briefing is short and obviously does not violate any of the confidentiality between the agency and company. It is extremely important; if the agency does not volunteer such a briefing, you should insist on it. The briefing should prepare you for what to expect during the interview. The briefing usually includes a short background of the company, a recent company annual report, a history of the job, a description of the company environment and the executive(s) involved in the interview, and any pertinent aspects or peculiarities. This briefing is so critical that you should be very cautious about using an agency that does not provide one.

Some agencies do not belong to any network but operate with one office or several offices in neighboring regions. This type of agency obviously does not provide a link-up with a national network, but it is in no way limited to placing applicants only in the areas where its offices are maintained. The agency usually has contacts either within a certain specific industrial category—for example, the computer industry—or within a certain job classification (comptrollers throughout a wide geographic area, for example). In addition, this type of agency usually is highly personalized and gives the applicant excellent service, particularly in areas of career counseling and company briefings. Indeed, it can be particularly effective because previously satisfied applicants become the present and future employers.

An organization that greatly aids MBAs in securing a broad range of positions outside of an immediate locale is the National Personnel Associates. Formed in 1957 in Chicago, NPA is the world's largest placement system for MBA-level jobs. The organization consists of approximately 250 offices in over 150 metropolitan areas, through which over 600,000 placements have been made. Through this network an employer in Dallas can find an MBA candidate in Boston. Similarly, an MBA with no geographic restrictions and perhaps a very specialized interest can be placed through an NPA member even though no opportunity exists in the applicant's present geographic area. The match takes place either by telephone between NPA members or with résumés and cover sheet sent by the NPA to its members. This mailing can be sent out selectively to member agencies by geographical region, selected Standard Industrial Classification code, or vocational codes such as sales or nationally to all members. For example, an MBA who was working in sales for a major photographic company in Boston wanted to work in sales in California. Therefore her résumé and cover sheet were sent to affiliate agencies in California who deal with sales.

This nationwide network allows both the employer and the applicant the widest possible exposure. While the company is given a nationwide listing of possible candidates to screen, the MBA has the opportunity to match his or her résumé with job openings across the country. The fee is a percent of the annual starting salary; it is paid by the employer. When multiple agencies are involved, the fee is divided between the agency supplying the job and the agency supplying the candidate, with the NPA central organization receiving a 5 percent brokerage fee. For more information on NPA write to its headquarters:

National Personnel Associates
150 Fountain NE
Grand Rapids, MI 49503

In addition to the NPA, another organization provides nationwide coverage for the MBA through a network of about 2,400 private employment agencies. This is the National Association of Personnel Consultants (NAPC). Founded in Milwaukee in 1937, originally to obtain salespeople from other areas, NAPC was a pioneer in nationwide private employment placement. NAPC works in basically the same manner as NPA. Once a résumé enters an agency it achieves nationwide distribution to all member agencies of NAPC. Further information on NAPC can be obtained by writing to its headquarters:

National Association of Personnel Consultants
1012 14th Street NW
Washington, DC 20006

A Note About Executive Search Firms

There is often confusion concerning the difference between employment agencies and executive search firms. An executive search firm is basically a consulting firm hired by a company to locate a candidate for a particular executive position. Often these assignments originate from a management study that indicates some organizational changes are needed. Usually payment is made by the company for professional services rendered regardless of whether a candidate is actually hired. The executive search company usually carefully evaluates the client company, its personnel environment, and its objectives in order to understand the functions to be performed and the attributes needed for the person sought. From this analysis, the search firm locates qualified candidates. If a person is interested in the opening, then a meeting is arranged. In short, executive search firms recruit only executives at high salary levels and represent the company seeking that executive talent. There is more on executive search firms in the next chapter.

When to Use Agency

In developing a job campaign, you should understand how an employment agency may or may not fit into your plans. Look at the benefits an agency provides. First, an agency has a wide range of opportunities on a widely diverse industry and geographic basis; it therefore provides a wider range of available positions than is normally the case. Second, the agency can save valuable time. One of the keys to a successful job campaign is to maximize time by putting your most effort into areas that have the highest probability of payback. An effective employment agency can do some initial screening and eliminate the time spent interviewing companies; the only time you spend is in the selection of the agency and the initial agency interview. Third, an employment agency (particularly those in a network or with wide geographic contacts) can absorb some of the costs of the job campaign. While, as previously mentioned, you should not cut costs in the job search, an agency can absorb some of the "advertising" and telephone costs associated with a successful campaign. Fourth, an agency may have knowledge of positions that are not available from any other source. Some firms, owing to the confidential nature of the position or the personnel involved, only list their opening with an agency. Therefore only when qualified candidates are located will the position become known within the company as well as throughout the industry. Similarly, the confidentiality of the MBA is preserved when needed. Finally, an agency can offer a broad base of experience. Not only can the agency guide you to opportunities consistent with your interest, abilities, and qualifications, but it can also provide some important ancillary services in terms of résumé development, interviewing, and career counseling and advisement.

Choosing an Agency

Of course the critical step is to choose the best agency. To make it easier, break it down into a three-step process: determine the agencies dealing with your career field; select a well-run agency; and choose an agency counselor.

By now you will have chosen your career field. Agencies usually have some degree of specialization such as EDP, marketing, or finance. Therefore you will need to categorize all agencies in your area as to their field of expertise as well as their managerial level of placement.

From this classification, select one agency—or in some cases, two agencies. Particularly in large metropolitan areas, this can be a somewhat difficult task for there may appear to be dozens of qualified agencies. It is important, then, to be able to recognize a well-run agency: one that operates efficiently and effectively, and consequently has substantial results. But how does one recognize a well-run agency?

There are several signs that indicate a superior agency. First, the agency must operate in a systematic, professional, and business-like manner. Every contact with the agency, from the secretary to the president, should indicate that this is the operating procedure and environment of the firm. Second, a good agency will take the time and effort needed to get to know and understand you; a poorly run agency in its effort to hold down costs will cut corners by spending less time in interviewing and classifying applicants. An efficient agency attempts to maximize the match; it does not send the seeking company dozens of candidates under the theory that the greater the number, the more likely the probability that someone will be hired. Finally, a quality agency attempts to help you locate the opportunity that best fits your goals. This sometimes entails career counseling and always involves extensive explanation of the company and its position before each interview.

Once the correct agency is determined, it is important to

select the most appropriate counselor at the agency. In general an employment agency is only as effective as its counselors; an effective counselor is so important that if one is not available in the agency you select, move to another agency. The counselor has the responsibility of determining the best position and company environment. Because this match is so critical, your counselor/applicant relationship should become a close, almost intimate one. Through this close working relationship, a good agency can indeed play a major role in the MBA's successful job campaign. A list of employment agencies in selected metropolitan areas can be found in Appendix II.

10

Executive
Search Firms

$\mathbf{A}$s indicated in the previous chapter, executive search firms (often called executive recruiters or executive consulting services), are somewhat related to the employment agencies. Table 10-1 is a comparison of the two as far as employment level, salary level, representation, fee structure, and scope of operation. As indicated, an executive search firm is hired by a company to obtain the best individual for an executive-level position. As such, executive search is essentially a management consulting function, in which the financial arrangement established between the firm and the client company is dependent somewhat on the services offered.

Executive search consultants (or "head hunters," as they are commonly called) have grown significantly in both reputation and competency since their inception in the late 1940s. At that time, as well as during the early 1950s, executive search firms generally operated with little or no expertise and questionable ethics. Today the firms still in existence have eliminated most of these negative connotations and have formed a thriving and important avenue for MBA career changes.

It is estimated that U.S. companies presently spend about $180 million per year for professional recruiting services. About 10,000

TABLE 10-1 Comparison of Employment Agencies and Executive Search Firms

Areas	Employment Agencies	Executive Recruiters
Employment level	Recruit at all levels from entry position to executives	Recruit executives only
Salary level	Placements usually cluster around lower management salary range: $25,000–$40,000	Placements generally cluster at upper level salary ranges $50,000 and up
Representation	Represent both the job seeker and the company on a contingent fee basis	Represent the company
Fee structure	Almost always paid entirely by company	Always paid by company (the fee is usually about 20%–30% of positions annual salary plus expenses)
Scope of operation	Usually have a fully staffed office with interviewing personnel and secretary	Vary from an answering service, one-person operation to a fully-staffed, attractive location

to 14,000 managerial jobs are filled each year by this method through approximately 1,000 executive search firms. You'll find a list of search firms located in major metropolitan areas in Appendix III. While executive recruiters cover all ranges of middle and upper-level management positions, they concentrate on spots commanding annual salaries over $50,000. At this upper range search firms deal with some of the largest corporations and top corporate jobs, many of which involve six-figure salaries. Emphasis on high salaries is one characteristic that sets executive search firms apart from employment agencies. Executive search firms also—as the name implies—recruit only executives; employment agencies recruit at all levels. Executive search firms range in size from a one-person office to being staffed by many individuals; they always represent the company. Employment agencies, on the other hand, usually have a fully staffed office with interviewing personnel, and they represent both the job seeker and the company. The fee for executive recruiting is always paid by the company; employment agencies are almost always paid entirely by the company.

Search Process

While the basic search process developed by the recruiter depends on the company and the management level, there are some common activities. The first step a recruiting firm takes after receipt of an assignment is to visit the client company. The recruiter attempts to understand everything about the job so that the firm can find the appropriate individual. A good executive search firm's future business is based on its reputation of successful placement; it cannot afford to place a candidate in a position where he or she will not be a success. Information is gathered on how the need for an outside executive arose, the job requirements, the credentials and personality characteristics required, and the basic organizational network. Based on this information, the executive recruiter prepares as exhaustive and detailed a job description as possible, which includes all information that has not been deemed confidential by the company. Now the actual search process begins, and potential MBA candidates are contacted, usually by telephone. Any candidate showing interest is sent the job description. If, after the analysis of this job description, the MBA candidate is still interested, he or she is asked to fill out a detailed standard employment form indicating background, qualifications, and work experience. A this point, the MBA candidate does not know the name of the client and the company does not know the MBA's name. This exchange of names does not usually occur until the last step in the search process, when the credentials of four to five MBA candidates are sent to the company.

After the search firm has the background information on the MBA, there is an exhaustive personal interview. Through this process the recruiter attempts to determine the most appropriate candidates to introduce to the client company. Sometimes an extensive psychological test is given, however most executive recruiters acknowledge that 75 to 80 percent of their evaluations of a candidate stem from the personal interview, not from testing. Expert interviewing is so important a part of the process that an MBA should in turn get a feel for the quality and professionalism of the search firm during this interview.

More general information on executive search firms and their operations can be obtained from:

The Association of Executive Recruiting
Consultants Inc. (AERC)
30 Rockefeller Plaza
New York, New York 10020

Usefulness for MBA

Executive recruiters are only useful to MBAs who are currently employed and performing well in their present position. Most firms are not interested in interviewing MBAs who are not performing well. For unemployed MBAs, the employment agency is the better avenue of approach; contacting an executive search firm would only waste valuable time and effort.

Many search firms are not interested in receiving unsolicited résumés from MBAs, even those who are in a good present position. The résumé tends to indicate to the executive recruiter that the MBA is not happy and not operating effectively, and, therefore, may also be unhappy in a new position. Executive recruiters actively seek potential applicants, thus sending a résumé contradicts their basic function. Should you work with a recruiter, keep in mind that the recruiter—more than the employment agency—works for the company. Remember that you are very happy and progressing rapidly in your present position. The only information you seek from that executive recruiter is what aspects of that new position make the recruiter think you would be interested in it. Why should you be interested in changing, and what can they offer you that you don't have now?

Should you choose to utilize a search firm, the time to register is while you are happily and rapidly progressing in a solid career track. Through this "token registration" the executive search firm can get to know you at your best. When some future job opportunity arises, the search firm may remember you first. Register with several search firms, with particular emphasis on those where you have first spoken with someone in the firm and feel most comfortable. In these initial exploratory dealings, as well as in all subsequent ones, you must be totally open.

In addition to the token registration, it is wise to contact an executive recruiter when you learn that the recruiter is seeking an individual for a specific position for which you are qualified. When this does occur, you should mention that position, so that the recruiter immediately associates it with you. If an offer for the position does not follow, at least your résumé is on file and another match might occur for the next position. It is, of course, much better to contact the recruiter as a response to a specific job opening than unsolicited one; therefore be aware of any recruiting taking place and respond while you're in a successful career path.

It is also particularly beneficial to list with an executive recruiter when you have specific skills, interests, or experience that correspond with the general field in which the recruiter operates. For example, if you are in investment banking and a recruiting firm operates in that field, send an introductory letter and résumé for future possibilities. These recruiters for specific fields have a greater tendency to file résumés for future job opportunities.

As previously indicated, the key to any dealings with executive recruiters—whether on a solicited or unsolicited basis—is an initial understanding that you are very happy and successful in your present position. The only reason for contacting a recruiter is to see if there is an even more advanced or challenging position—a faster track—available.

Services Provided to the Company

In order to benefit from an executive search firm, you should understand completely the services they provide the companies they represent. These can be categorized into three general areas: as a personnel consultant, for analysis of job requirements, and as a source of candidates. Of these areas, the one which will bring most positive results is as a personnel consultant. Most executive recruiters are so experienced that they are able not only to identify any problems related to the position but also to help eliminate problems that may occur in filling the position. In this respect it is imperative that the company inform the recruiter of all aspects of the job, including problems. The only way a successful placement can occur is if the recruiter/company relationship is open and frank, on a confidential basis similar to the relationship a doctor or lawyer has with a client. The company can never be too specific. For example, one company was having a difficult time finding a marketing research manager. It finally came out that the vice-president of marketing did not think anyone who smoked a pipe or wore bow ties was competent and aggressive.

The company should provide the recruiter with a thorough, in-depth briefing on the firm and its environment. This is particularly important when the position is a top managment one with very broad job responsibilities. It is also important to identify basic corporate attitudes or philosophies—in other words, whether the company is aggressive or conservative, family-owned or controlled, or a leader or follower in the industry. Also, the company should indicate the working conditions and social obligations of the job. One company had an unwritten policy that all company executives put in an informal hour or two almost every Saturday morning. Another company so dominated the small town in which it was operating that each executive was not only expected to live in the town but in a particular section of the town depending on the level of management.

The second major service provided by the recruiter for the company is to give a detailed description of the job—its requirements and its specifications. While the company prepares an initial job description, this first effort is expanded as needed. It is rare that at least some expansion and change is not made in the initial job description. Of course, one key to successful placement is a clear, concise job description.

In addition to the actual job description, the recruiter is helpful in establishing the salary and benefits package, as well as making any changes in the job title or reporting relationships.

The final service an effective executive recruiting firm provides a company is, of course, a rich source of well-qualified candidates. The company in return suggests any known sources of candidates. If applicable, the company identifies any other companies from which they will not recruit, as well as industry policies on executive transfers among companies.

Characteristics of a Good Search Firm

As was the case with the selection of an employment agency, it is important that you be involved with the best possible recruiting firm. Little capital investment is required to enter the executive-recruiting field, and this dilutes the number of excellent firms available. Of the 1,000 operating in the United States, too many do not measure up to high standards. How, then, does one distinguish among firms?

Track record is an indication, but that is not conclusive. Placement history must be cautiously viewed and never used exclusively, since even the most professional or successful recruiters fill only 80 percent of their searches. This 20 percent failure rate is often because the company later decided against filling the position, salary was too low, or a candidate from another source was more suitable for the position. This is the case even though top search firms only accept assignments they feel reasonably capable of filling; they usually take assignments only in fields they have familiarity with.

In order to evaluate executive recruiting firms, we've provided a checklist; see Table 10-2. Rate each firm on a scale from 1 to 7, with 1 being poor and 7 being excellent. In this way, you can feel that you are using the best possible recruiting firm.

MBAs Dealing with a Search Firm

It is reasonable to expect that several times in your career you will get a call from an executive recruiter. The telephone call

TABLE 10-2 Rating Scales for an Executive Recruiting Firm

Criteria	Poor	Moderate	Excellent	Not Able to Evaluate
	Name of Firm			
Length of time in business	1 2	3 4 5	6 7	8
Physical appearance of office	1 2	3 4 5	6 7	8
Location of office(s)	1 2	3 4 5	6 7	8
Number of offices	1 2	3 4 5	6 7	8
Type and size of staff	1 2	3 4 5	6 7	8
Types of previous clients	1 2	3 4 5	6 7	8
Types of previous placements	1 2	3 4 5	6 7	8
Ability to specify job	1 2	3 4 5	6 7	8
Ability in evaluating candidates	1 2	3 4 5	6 7	8
Refers few candidates to client company	1 2	3 4 5	6 7	8
Works closely with client company	1 2	3 4 5	6 7	8
Good capability at establishing salary package	1 2	3 4 5	6 7	8
Proper professional fee structure	1 2	3 4 5	6 7	8
Professionalism and maturity of personnel	1 2	3 4 5	6 7	8

always comes at your office, at which time the recruiter identifies him or herself and the recruiting firm, gives a brief general description of the company and position, and asks you if you know of anyone who might be interested in an opening. The recruiter expects that if you are interested, you will position yourself at the top of the list, if indeed any list is forthcoming at all. This phone call obviously places you in a dilemma: Is the call a hoax? Is the person at the other end trustworthy? Will the response affect your current position? What exactly is the best response?

In order both to avoid any embarrassment or damage to your present job and to give you time to think about the position and to talk freely at your leisure, always suggest returning the call. This response can be made without giving any indication of interest. During the return call, be extremely cautious, yet courteous. Since executive recruiters are experienced on the telephone, they are very sensitive to any underlying messages in your voice or manner.

Obviously, as previously indicated, do not appear too anxious. However, even if not interested, learn about the position. This may be the basis for establishing a relationship with the recruiter that may lead to a successful position match the next time. At the very least it may allow you to recommend a friend for the current position. Even if you have some interest, still do not appear overly interested, and allow the recruiter to suggest the time and place for the next meeting. The next meeting should be face-to-face, probably over lunch so that you can sense the professionalism of the recruiter.

In assessing the executive recruiter, use the checklist previously discussed (see Table 10-2); exercise great care if the recruiter mentions the company's name or is too specific too soon about the nature of the position. Details of the position are usually not discussed until much later in the process. Call off the entire process immediately if the executive recruiter even hints at any payment from you; the fee is always paid by the company hiring the recruiter. During this time, inquire about the size of the company, its organization, and the general nature of the position; ask the recruiter to send a written specification of the job to your home. This allows you further time to evaluate the position and its merits without any time pressures or constraints. In addition, the job description can indicate the professional level of the recruiting firm.

Once you indicate some interest, the "wooing posture" of the executive recruiter is replaced by a hard-core evaluative one. The recruiter will arrange a meeting for an in-depth interview so that he or she can determine your qualifications. The company for whom the search is being made may still not be identified, since the recruiter is interviewing numerous candidates for the position. If this initial screen is a positive one, the executive recruiter will discreetly check you out with former employers and subordinates as well. The recruiter will check all possible references, while being careful not to jeopardize your present position. After this exhaustive search, if you are one of the four or five final candidates, then you'll hear the name of the company and a company interview will be set up.

The Company Interview

Before the company interview, it is imperative that you do the necessary homework. Find out everything possible about the company, or else do not waste the time attending the interview. In some instances, the interview is scheduled immediately after the company is identified. If this occurs, explain at the beginning of the interview that there was insufficient time to prepare.

During the actual interview, take every opportunity to sell yourself. Keep in mind: "If you don't toot your own horn, your horn never blows." There are perfect opportunities for doing this as you respond to questions. As a general rule of thumb, always give more information in response to a question than is required. But take particular care before beginning your answer to such an open-ended question, because these questions are the opportunities for selling yourself.

Sometimes, particularly at higher level positions, the company interview can follow some unusual formats. For example, one company asked each candidate to prepare an agenda for the meeting by developing key questions that should be asked. The candidate is then queried on how the list was established and what the rationale was.

Another company gave MBA candidates a general problem or situation in the company. The MBA's notes on the problem provided the basis for most of the discussion. Yet another company had each MBA candidate meet with two company officials who had opposite views on a particular topic. The candidates were evaluated on their abilities to deal with the differences of opinion.

A final interviewing technique used by several companies is to have each candidate think of himself or herself as a consultant to the company and to develop some recommendations to solve a problem. This technique is employed by many companies because it allows them to assess whether you understand the situation and can develop sensible recommendations based on the available data.

During the interview, do not start talking salary too soon. If the company is interested in you, it will pay what it takes to hire you away from your current position. In this regard, take care not to ask "small" questions regarding such things as vacation policies or retirement benefits. These are generally standard in the final negotiation process. In terms of the final salary package, be careful not to place too many conditions on accepting the offer. Also, never ask for a contract.

Regardless of the type of interview employed, if an offer is forthcoming, ask for time to consider it. Never worry about the company's retracting the offer; if the company wants you it will wait a reasonable amount of time to ensure that your decision is a firm and wise one.

While it is of course appropriate, never say "I would like to discuss this offer with my spouse." Even if you value the opinion of your spouse, don't give the company the impression that your husband or wife influences your decisions.

Once you accept the position, always ask for a letter from the company outlining the job, its responsibilities, and the complete salary package. This will ensure that no misunderstandings have occurred. When a starting date is agreed upon, make sure you are ready to start on that date. Your primary loyalty should be to the new company and its position, not to the company you are leaving. There is no reason to begin a job on the wrong basis by failing to live up to this first initial promise, and you should make whatever compromises are necessary to satisfy this commitment.

11

Which Job Do I Take?

If you plan your job strategy as outlined in this book, you will probably have at least two good job offers and as many as four or five. This is an enviable position. With this opportunity, however, also comes the responsibility of choosing among them to arrive at the best decision for both the short and long run. To make this choice, consider several factors, and keep in mind that it is as important for you to be completely comfortable with your new job as it is for the company to want you to join it. For total job success, the two go hand in hand.

Your Criteria

Your first consideration is, which company is strongest? Which is moving forward on the most solid foundation? Which company is in the healthiest industry? Which company serves demographics that show growth potential? For example, secondary school systems are likely to have severe problems in the 1980s. Similarly, the American automotive industry does not offer the same potential for good health as it did in the 1950s and 1960s. Retail department stores are currently losing a share of their market to direct mail merchandising and other nonstore retailing. You must take a hard look at the company and its growth, its current position, and where its world is heading.

How do you go about doing it? Once again you must do some research, but even more carefully this time. Go to the library and also write or call trade associations. Obtain as much demographic and financial data as possible. Talk to faculty and industry people close to the company (or companies) you are considering. Look at all the financial data on companies who have offered you a position. Carefully analyze the markets that these companies are serving. What is their growth potential? Is the company diversified enough to withstand an economic drought in the parent industry? Talk to competitors. Speak with consumers who use the products and distribution outlets who handle both the company's products as well as competing ones. And, most importantly, try to talk to MBAs who already work for your prospective company or competing ones. Particularly, talk with alumni from your school.

Business as well as personal decisions are made based on explicit criteria. You must develop your criteria for selecting a company. It is also good to ask executives in the companies which have offered you a position—and specifically your prospective boss—why they chose to work for that firm. What were the criteria they used and what led to their company choice? Also, what do they see as the company's strengths and weaknesses? Try to get a feeling for the atmosphere in the company and its possible personality fit. And, of course, always send thank-you letters to everyone with whom you speak.

Executive recruiters may be able to provide a less biased viewpoint about the company than company personnel and friends, particularly with respect to the relative advantages and disadvantages of each job. Ask the recruiters what value your experience will have on the market should you decide to leave one company for another. Most recruiters are usually willing to spend ten or fifteen minutes on the telephone with you. The recruiter may some day place you in another position. Even more importantly, the recruiter may talk to you another day as a prospective employer for one of his or her clients. Indeed, executive recruiters have a vested interest in staying in touch with you. They also like to keep abreast of salaries and openings at the entry level. Contacts in industry are their biggest asset.

What Does the Company Stand For?

Finally, and perhaps most importantly, you need to determine if the company will meet your personal and professional needs. How progressive is the company? How concerned? The following is a realistic set of expectations you should have about your first post-MBA job.

1. The job should give you a sense of meaning or goals and the accompanying status and prestige.

2. There should be ample opportunity for personal and professional development, challenge, and responsibility.

3. The position should offer interesting work that triggers curiosity and creates excitement.

4. Management should offer recognition and approval for good work. There should be feedback and a carefully monitored evaluation system.

5. The salary should be fair and have a reasonable amount of growth opportunity and security.

6. The company should be "friendly."

7. There should be careful attention to your training.

Similarly, there are certain things the company will expect from an MBA. You should:

1. Be able to learn various aspects of a position while on the job.

2. Be able to develop new methods of performing tasks and solving unusual problems.

3. Be able to work productively with others in groups.

4. Be able to supervise others.

5.   Be able to make sound decisions and communicate these both verbally and in writing.

6.   Be able to organize your own work load and that of others.

7.   Be willing to accept company demands when they conflict with personal plans.

8.   Want to pursue continuing education after regular working hours.

9.   Contribute to maintaining a good company image.

10.   Feel comfortable with most company values and goals.

After interviewing fifteen to twenty-five companies, you will develop very sophisticated criteria. Some offers will not fit your personal goals. Important issues will gradually come into focus, and day-to-day fluctuations in your thinking will diminish. Be sure to take the time to make the correct decision.

Choice Techniques

One technique that you might try if you are having a particularly difficult time deciding between two job offers is to flip a coin, then measure your regret at having foregone the other offer. Live with the decision for a day, then change the decision in favor of the other company the next day and again measure the regret. The objective is to minimize your regret, and this technique may bring some previously unconsidered issues to light.

Sometimes even after a variety of techniques are employed, there is still no apparent "right" choice. In this situation, try to decide what is most important to you. For example, suppose you decide the medium- and long-term opportunities at each of three companies are equivalent. In addition, the experience with any one of the three companies would provide an excellent background should you decide to leave. Since all these are the same, the first-year experience is the most important variable. At this point, call an executive in your functional area at each of the three companies and talk about that first-year experience. Make some direct comparisons that would not otherwise have been possible, particularly since the interviews at the different companies were separated by time. Other possibilities to help in your decision-making dilemma include:

❦ Asking for an extension in time if there is a good reason for extending the deadline for your response to a company's offer.

❦ Making a visit to a company on your own after the interviewing is completed. This visit allows you to interview people in a more relaxed atmosphere, but gives you another look at the area you may be living in.

❦ Using intuition in your decision among a limited number of final offers. When logic does not work, it may be time to be emotional. Factors that do not make much sense to anyone but you may take on new importance.

After making a decision, be sure to let the other companies know your decision immediately. These companies have spent a lot of time and money recruiting you, and they deserve to be treated with the same professional courtesy as you received from them. Not only that, but the companies you say "no" to now represent career opportunities in the future should you decide to switch jobs.

Salary Negotiations

One of the most difficult aspects of the decision is salary. In this negotiation, even more than in any other, you must feel good about yourself; you must be confident about all your attributes and accomplishments which led to the job offer in the first place.

As an MBA, you must be scrupulous and thorough when discussing salary. The time to negotiate the best salary offer is before you accept an offer, not after. Remember that any good employer respects a tough but fair negotiator, and an example of how effective a negotiator you will be for the company is reflected in how you negotiate your own affairs. Be very demanding with yourself. Do your research carefully, develop your position, and plan on bargaining.

Of course, not every MBA gets the same starting salary. It

is also not necessarily true that a Harvard Business School MBA would get more than an MBA from Ohio State. You must develop an idea of what the best possible deal would be for you; once you reach a realistic minimum, negotiate very strategically.

A shrewdly developed salary negotiation indicates to the employer your flexibility, your art of preparation, your intelligent toughness, and your understanding of finance. The better you are at this, the more assured an employer is that you are going to handle the company's affairs competently. While the personnel manager may argue the salary range with you, he or she will be pleased with your ability to bargain.

It's important to establish as early as possible what the salary range is. You should know the range, not the exact salary of previous MBAs employed there, and if the salary you prefer is beyond the company's range, you are wasting your time and energy negotiating for the impossible. If there is doubt in your mind regarding other MBAs' salaries, talk to your placement office, your dean, or your faculty or try to get in touch with people you know in comparable programs. Do not push too hard, but also do not retreat too quickly. There is no better way to judge the sincerity, management style, and business competence of a prospective employer than by how the salary negotiation is handled. The final salary must be comfortable to *both* you and the company.

Salary should be negotiated every twelve to eighteen months. Avoid six-month reviews if you can. Not only are six-month reviews inconclusive, they put an individual under too much pressure to achieve too quickly. And salary increments should be based on solid accomplishment. For example, if you start at $25,000, it would not be unreasonable for you to be making $30,000 in two years. After you negotiate eighteen- to twenty-four month possible increments, indicate to your employer that if those types of raises are not forthcoming, you will assume it is an indication you are not performing and should seek employment elsewhere.

Raises negotiated in advance provide both parties with a clearly defined criterion for appraising performance. And establishing a future at the beginning implies your long-term commitment to the company. If your prospective employer is unwilling to discuss future raises, you will have to decide whether to continue considering this employer. Sometimes it is shrewd to settle for a lower starting salary arrangement if you are guaranteed future increments on the basis of good performance. Being willing to offer present against future gains can be very attractive to employers.

The following are some general principles to follow in salary negotiations:

1.   Do not sell yourself too low, and be sure to know the entire details of the final salary package. If you come in too high the company will not meet your demands; if you come in too low the company could in fact lose interest. Always come in near the top of the company's range in your starting minimum. This gives you an excellent opportunity to increase the final salary even more.

2.   Rigorously research what comparable MBAs are obtaining. One excellent source of information is *Paychecks: Who Makes Them*, by David Harrop. The book gives information on what individuals at various levels earn. The college placement council also publicizes salary information, available through your library or career placement office. The *Occupational Outlook Handbook* has salary information; many industries have associations which keep salary information. When conducting this research, be careful to isolate salary information for your particular geographic area.

3.   Always negotiate with a salary range in mind and attempt to finalize a salary at the top end of the range. Attempt to determine salary ranges of individuals above and below you in the organization. Former employees, people in competing organizations, and annual reports can be helpful in providing this information.

4.   Future raises are as much a part of the compensation package as the starting salary package or promotions. Both should be discussed at the time of the initial salary negotiation.

5.   Do not feel guilty about asking for more money. Always ask for more than you are worth, more than the company is willing to pay, and more than you expect the employer to offer. Remember you have more leverage regarding compensation *before* you take the job than *after*.

6. Do not back the salary negotiator into a corner. Just state what you want, then be flexible to the extent needed. Always indicate flexibility without weakness. Establish your maximum request and negotiate to the midpoint.

7. Rarely does salary hinder the final hiring process. The hard part of the negotiation is already over; the company wants you and you want it. When you give the employer a salary figure, always indicate the reasons behind it, such as education, experience, acquired knowledge, accomplishments and motivation. Remember that your salary is in part based on the salary you made or would have made upon graduation from college plus the salary increments and the monetary value of your MBA.

8. Never indicate why you need money. These are your problems, not the employer's. Bargaining from need is not a competent strategy.

9. There is no simple formula for determining what should be your final salary.

10. If you have more than one job offer, let each company quietly know that you have more than one offer. However, do not overtly reveal one company's identity to the other.

11. Do not hesitate to "sleep on" an offer to gain perspective.

12. Always indicate tactfully to the company that because you capably represent your own interests well in negotiating for a position you will be able to represent the company's interests similarly upon employment.

13. If asked (and only if asked) in a first interview, always describe your salary needs as negotiable.

14. Even if money is not crucial to you, always press for what you are worth. Yet, as important as income is,

keep in mind the psychological pluses of a position. You will earn your salary if your performance is outstanding. If it is not, you will not be in the job long.

15. When possible, tie your salary to projected productivity. However, do not accept a bonus as a large part of your remuneration unless you are in a position personally to influence its size by what you do, and you are confident that you can achieve the expected results.

16. Remember you have the same salary opportunity no matter from which MBA program you graduated. Your final salary depends largely on how shrewdly you interview and negotiate.

17. Ask for an employment letter. Such a letter should indicate the details of employment. Be sure provisions for continuing evaluation are specified.

Other Fringe Benefits

Even for MBAs just starting, there is more to a job than just the straight salary. Money frequently is just one part of the total compensation, and there are significant other elements to consider. Obtain a complete description of the compensation package. If a company really wants you, they may be very flexible in these other areas. Most MBAs, particularly those from schools other than the top ten, have no idea how much can be negotiated in the area of other benefits. Listed below are some things you should consider. While not all are available in every company, they should at least be discussed in the salary negotiation.

INCOME

1. Salary

2. Bonuses

3. Commissions

4. Stock options at a future time (these are once again in

vogue because of recent favorable changes in the tax law)

5. Profit-sharing plans

6. Deferred profit sharing held in trust

7. Deferred compensation

BENEFITS

1. Moving expenses

2. Pension plan

3. Health insurance beyond Blue Cross, Blue Shield

4. Dental insurance plan

5. Sick pay

6. Accident insurance

7. Group life insurance

8. Death allowance

9. Vacations and leaves of absence

10. Down payment on a house

BONUSES

1. Expense account

2. Credit cards

3. Club memberships

4. Company automobile

5. Paid parking

6. Day-care facilities

STATUS

    1.   Attractive office

    2.   Secretary

The Closing

It's very important in any final salary closing to be certain that both the company and you understand the final terms. This is not a time for any misunderstanding. Rigorous attention to details will not be interpreted as a lack of confidence in the company's financial integrity. Whenever possible, negotiate for what you require; do not just accept what you are offered.

Basically most job offers involve a mixture of four ingredients: money, benefits, prequisites, and status. Each is usually negotiable. Sometimes it may be advisable to obtain an accountant's advice on the maximum value of each, but in the last analysis you have to trust your own judgment. Obtaining the best possible package is the culmination of your entire campaign and should be very satisfying to both you and the company. The company is pleased because they are getting who they wanted; you are pleased because you are getting what you want. If all the factors described in this chapter are in your final offer, the effort of getting your MBA degree will have been worth it. Work hard and enjoy a rewarding career!

12

Special MBA Problems

Although the preceding chapters are relevant to any MBA, there are some career problems that confront a few special groups: women, minority group members, dual-career couples, MBAs from less prestigious schools, and those for whom the MBA represents a career change. Let's look at each situation.

Women MBAs

Change is slow in the workplace. Even today some women entering business will face barriers to their career progress. After all, in some corporate headquarters if a woman is seen at a meeting, she is still presumed to be a secretary. Women remain at a severe numerical disadvantage with their male peers. In some organizations, she is the token woman, and her role is very similar to the lone black executive in a white corporate hierarchy.

Many male executives discuss women in sexist terms, and women in sales particularly are the subject of conversation, questions, gossip, and scrutiny. Any deviation from normal behavior will create conversation and a woman generally will not have as much freedom and cannot be as independent. Women also can afford fewer mistakes.

They have to be careful how they conduct themselves and what they say to other managers. Women MBAs have had the same training as men, yet they have fewer of the traditional advantages afforded men in similar situations.

Historically, males found their way to the best jobs, even in occupations where many women held junior and middle management positions. What's more, the number of women managers actually decreased during the 1960s and 1970s. Today, when there are more women MBAs, they tend to have positions with less visibility. This lack of visibility usually means less credit for accomplishments, and—in a self-perpetuating way—fewer promotions. Since women managers tend also to have positions with less client or marketplace contact, they are not usually considered in the fast track. When MBA women are promoted to higher-level positions, those spots frequently do not lead to further top management responsibilities but rather to senior-level staff jobs. And chief executive officers usually do not emerge from staff positions, regardless of the level.

In some companies, in order to rise in the chain of command, women must not only meet the performance criteria set for their male counterparts, but must actually rise above those standards. The MBA woman needs to remember constantly that it is not know-how alone that brings promotions. But if she looks for the same opportunities as a male MBA, she may be viewed as pushy and lacking managerial finesse. On the other hand, if she stays too low keyed, she is likely to be seen as "not interesting."

If you are extremely competent—an overachiever—you must be very diplomatic, lest you give male executives the feeling they are being invaded by a high-achieving woman. Invisibility is a safer posture, since the male ego is not challenged, however this has the high cost of limited recognition and career growth.

There are no written rules governing women in business. Often accomplishments and knowledge are not deciding factors for advancement; instead, subjective criteria become the basis for a woman's growth and success. There are, however, the informal rules of business which women should understand and can put to their advantage. Learning how the "system" works is part of the job—one which women have traditionally ignored. For example, women often do not mingle and socialize as do their male counterparts, and this often hampers their ability to operate effectively and efficiently within the organization, especially in an informal structure. As women strive for positions of increasingly higher caliber, they need to use the system even more. Gaining access to traditional male jobs is a difficult task, but you can do it by manipulating the system, not by allowing yourself to be manipulated by it.

Most important, women have to be unusually careful when starting out to select positions with managers who will let them grow. This is particularly important for the first position. Of course, nothing succeeds like success. If a woman establishes goals and develops a strategy, these goals can be achieved. The truly skillful MBA woman will obtain strategic management positions through creativity, willingness to take risks, motivation, and brilliant interpersonal skills. She will be forceful about her needs—to be seen and heard. And to get a good managerial job, she will have to show great commitment to the position and the company—in terms of time, emotion, personal relationships, and lifestyle. Of course, all this means that a woman must negotiate even more diligently for the proper salary, rank, career track, and office accommodations. Remember that MBA women still tend to lag behind men in starting salaries. But given the right organization, the woman MBA can move successfully up through the ranks.

Women MBAs are not expected by male employers to be big risk-takers. Therefore if a woman really wants to grow, she needs to indicate that she is a very good risk-taker. She must be prepared to be questioned about her motives, objectives, and management style. Her ability and depth of commitment will sometimes be questioned as well, and this can lead to doubts about herself and her destiny. A woman must constantly believe in her abilities and strive for ultimate success.

Aggressiveness on a woman's part is frequently not considered leadership, although it is in a man. Don't be misled by the egalitarian atmosphere of business school. In most MBA programs there are substantial numbers of women faculty, and male peers are used to women counterparts. But this is still not the case in many businesses. Some male executives even feel they are helping women executives by not burdening them with extra duties. This of course makes it difficult for the woman MBA to learn and grow. Whichever way you use, you'll have to get the attention of the business leaders, but if you are a fast track MBA, be careful to keep your flanks protected. You may need male support along the way.

Some other tips for women include:

1. Women MBAs, unless particularly interested, should stay away from positions in personnel, benefits, equal opportunities, and affirmative action or any other area which has come to be known as a bastion for women.

2. In time (although we have not seen this statistically tested) a woman's success will be more assured if there are a number of senior female executives in the company. This is something to consider in selecting a company and position.

3. Women MBAs with strong quantitative skills are in high demand at the present time.

4. It is not necessary to imitate men in manner and dress. Often it is much smarter to interview for a position in an attractive dress than in a tailored, three-piece, pinstripe suit.

Remember that as an MBA graduate, you have every right to expect and insist on equal treatment in the job marketplace and within the company.

Minority Group Members

Equitable career development in a company is not accidental. The management needs to be aware of the special problems minority group members face in order to provide such equality. There are class barriers and other differences in treatment that become readily apparent once an MBA is in the organization. In some less enlightened companies, the minority group MBA is forced to adopt a very assertive posture to get over these hurdles. Just having an MBA is not enough; the degree is not a guarantee for a top management position.

The higher you go in management, the more senior executives will view you objectively. Senior management is concerned with the bottom line, not the race of the individual. But getting to that level may be difficult unless the company is enlightened or you have a little help.

Minority MBAs even more than other groups need sponsors in the company to break down barriers. The sponsor will help a minority MBA to advance by spreading his or her reputation through the organization; the sponsor will bring the MBA to the attention of higher management when promotion opportunities arise, and will mention the MBA at management meetings.

As a minority group member you will have to decide whether or not to cling to your ethnic identity. Holding on to it may be difficult and even inhibiting in most companies, however rejecting it could be a real threat to your ego. Of course, some MBAs can use their background to their advantage. Many rank and file workers of all ethnic groups trust a well-educated executive with a strong ethnic identity and they crave leadership from him or her.

There are four most important points a minority MBA must consider. These are:

1. To determine how much ethnic background you want to retain. How comfortable will you be getting assimilated into the organization?

2. To consider how your family fits into your plans. You need to discuss whether retaining your ethnic background is important to them. How much ethnic culture is your family willing to relinquish?

3. To find a sponsor who is not a minority group member and ultimately seek a mentor who will provide perspective and help obtain visibility. This is necessary for every MBA, but perhaps even more critical for minorities.

4. To determine whether the company has a commitment to equality or simply engages in tokenism. Analyze the positions minorities presently hold and speak to them about their jobs.

Two-Career Couples

Only recently have major corporations become concerned about MBA couples. Many have even relaxed their rules regarding couples moving into management positions in the same company. The traditional personnel policies in several instances no longer meet the changing needs and problems in this world of working men and women. These companies have decided to do something about such two-career executives because without a change in corporate behavior some very good executives would be lost.

One problem that two-career couples face is that of relocation. One member will not move because the change will interfere with the career or studies of the other. Many young couples have a quality-of-life ethic that supercedes the more traditional success ethic, and things other than corporate success determine their decisions. Two-career couples generate the higher income helpful in maintaining this ethic, of course. For some MBA couples, the combined income brings them the security which permits them to be more aggressive and make their own career decisions. It permits them personal choice and an opportunity to avoid the corporate merry-go-round. The number of people involved in this two-career problem is significant. More than 50 million employed men and women, out of over 100 million in the American workforce, are now two-career couples. So this is a contemporary problem which will continue well into the future.

The questions that two-career couples must answer change as the years go by and as the people involved develop their careers. In the beginning, young couples usually try to avoid the potential problems, playing down questions of relocation or conflict of interest in interviews because a concern for such things might be interpreted as a lack of personal ambition or an unwillingness to make personal sacrifices. At this point also, most couples carefully analyze their situation and give each other mutual support and encouragement without viewing the longer-range situation. After all, at this point both have similar career needs. They have to develop their skills, gain experience, travel, and work long hours. They each have an intense commitment to their career goals. At this point, the major conflict might be some early pressure to relocate. Usually after some discussion, both partners show flexibility and develop a variety of solutions.

Later on in life, the two-career couple faces other problems. Often the needs of the careers conflict with the needs of the family. There are now more than just the two people to think of; there are children. The needs of the companies cease to be all-important, and the family's needs are more important. Also at this stage, questions of salary and location are very important. The man's career often conflicts with the wife's, and frequently the woman—who has made many of the concessions to date—is now unwilling to make more. Separation and divorce frequently result.

All is not so bleak, however. With the increasing age also comes increasing maturity and experience with decision-making. At this point, two-career couples are seasoned experts, and they should be able to cope with the problems. Once the family's needs are fixed, the career goals can become more flexible. Also, at this stage the partners are more willing to discuss their problems with their companies.

There are two important factors for two-career couples to keep in mind. The first is that each person should have a commitment to the other's career in addition to his or her own. This is easier said than done, of course, but the spouse's career can become a source of pride. Second, each partner has to develop devices for coping with the problems as they arise. This is best accomplished when:

❦ You maintain a flexibility about your job and your family. Compromise occasionally; reevaluate your goals to see if what you are pursuing is worth the conflict; consider your partner's point of view.

❦ Establish priorities for your work and leisure time, then organize your time so you accomplish your goals. Enlist outside help to carry out household chores and choose your leisure activities wisely.

When interviewing for positions, obtain complete job information and discover the viewpoints of the company regarding relocation and spouse involvement in decision-making. Plan your steps in advance and develop alternatives so that you have solutions at the ready for the problems as they arise. Seek out companies that are interested in two-career couples (many view them as more loyal), that are open to changes in work schedules, that allow extra benefits in terms of personal days, extra insurance, and vacation time; and that will help the partner find a new position should there be a need to relocate. In addition, ask the following about the companies you consider:

1. Does the company have flexible career development tracks?

2. Does the company understand the complexity of life/career management decisions?

3. Does the company have support services for two-career couples?

4. Is the company inclined to consider special work situations?

5. Does the company work with other firms in the area?

MBAs from Less Prestigious Schools

If you are not graduating from one of the top fifteen MBA schools (and most of you won't be), you will probably be asked why you did not go to one of these schools. The answer to this question provides a great deal of information for the interviewer. Why couldn't you get in? Did you make a mature decision? What criteria did you use in selecting a school?

It is always best to accent the positive and skim over or not mention the negative. Be assertive. Make a positive statement such as, "XYZ is an excellent school with a growing reputation. If offered the kind of curriculum I wanted and also had reputation for good professors: faculty who combine great classroom techniques with deep knowledge of their fields through research, publications, and consulting work in the field." Finally, discuss specifics to indicate the quality education you received from your school and how it has prepared you for a top job. The important thing is to be positive.

In the job market, it is likely you will have a more difficult time interesting employers in your capabilities. Most of the top MBA jobs are filled by people from the top schools. Yet you can compete with these graduates by setting a more aggressive job campaign with higher quality materials. An employer is often more impressed with a solid, aggressive job campaign than with the degree-granting institution. Positively indicate your accomplishments and your unique aspects which will be valuable to the company. Send high-quality correspondence that indicates the benefits that company will derive by employing you.

MBA Graduates Entertaining
Career or Job Change

There are many MBAs in their thirties who have painstakingly acquired an MBA on a part-time basis with a desire for a change in career, company, or job. Or another might be the person who left his or her job to attend a graduate business program full time.

These graduating MBAs are close to their peak of personal attainment. Their greater wisdom, experience, maturity, and a broadened education have come about through strong motivation and effort. In addition, their family, career, business colleagues, and personal friends have come into focus. Is it possible to take advantage of these attributes to expand the joys of life and to propel this executive to his or her highest level of professional accomplishment? It certainly is. Look at the many older people for whom later success was a consequence of earlier planning.

The formula for success in the mid to later years lies not only in work orientation but in physical health and psychological happiness. This is a period when executives start to face the reality of their professional lives, and frequently they see less attainment in their future years than they visualized when they began. A feeling of depression can follow, leading to frustration, a reduction in hope, and physical illness. Knowing that more and more top management positions are being filled by younger men and women makes the older MBA lose sight of personal and professional accomplishments, and that MBA will begin to think that the professional world is passing him or her by.

This is the time also when the older MBA graduate feels he or she has to keep moving to stay competitive. There is always the real or imagined threat of losing out to the competition, and there is always the feeling of dependence—on one's family and on one's company and subordinates.

This is the period when feelings about competing with peers, about satisfying the company, and about the need to be with your family develop. This is also the time which follows an intense work and/or school period which has drained everyone's patience. Instead of being able to take time for a respite, this person is in a state of readiness. While all this is occurring, the years are going by while the youthful vigor erodes.

Other changes are also taking place. The fire of creativity is turned toward carefully examined and formulated plans. The concern for organization becomes greater. These are, of course, positive attributes. But boredom, disillusionment, and a feeling of being burned out also occur during this period. An awareness that all is not loving and friendly may develop and divorce or serious family illness only tend to complicate life.

This too is a period when, despite all the work experience, wisdom, and skills, the executive frequently feels trapped—not in charge of his or her own destiny. The job pyramid becomes more difficult and restrictive, and the fight is not only for the next job but to stay ahead of the person who has just taken your previous job and might be performing it better. Youth appears to have all the things you never had. You start to realize that you are not immortal.

What does this all mean?

First, that it is perfectly normal to have feelings such as

those previously described. These usually occur after several years of business experience and after finishing a rigorous MBA program. The MBA may have taken up to five years to complete part time. Also, failure to recognize these feelings and do something about them may lead to severe problems later on.

Second, as a new, highly talented MBA graduate you should start immediately to develop a closer relationship with your family while developing new friendships. Get involved in some community concern—schools, colleges, and hospitals all need help! Start working hard at developing younger workers without fearing what they will take from you. If you take a radically new job, insist that a refresher program be established.

Above all, recognize your worth, your assets, look for a change that befits your years of education and experience. You now bring not only enhanced MBA skills but wisdom, maturity, and understanding to the position. This will make you an infinitely better manager.

Perhaps most important, look to mid-life—with all its problems and opportunities—to develop a type of professional and personal fulfillment which will be fulfilling in your 40s and 50s as well.

13

The First Year

The first year will be a time for learning; it should also be a year for personal and executive development. You must learn the routines, see how the priorities are set, and observe how the tasks are accomplished. Simultaneously, you should be seeking entry to management decision-making, recognizing that you are being closely scrutinized.

In the first year, you are primarily a subordinate who is learning. While it is more than just an apprenticeship, the first-year position does have some of the aspects of that. Building a relationship as a subordinate, working with a mentor who knows how to discern a problem, and analyzing and solving that problem within the organizational structure are activities that develop a solid foundation for the future. Accomplishing what the mentor directs can bring about his or her sponsorship of you. Your mentor can be very helpful in learning the ropes. A mentor is a role model, and finding a good mentor should be a priority for you.

Some MBAs feel that after completing a rigorous undergraduate and graduate education they are ready for independence. Then they suddenly realize on this first job that they are not only expected to willingly accept direction, but that their attempts at creativity and initiative are tightly supervised. After two years at school of solving complicated problems and cases, of playing president, and of looking forward to executive responsibilities, an MBA usually finds

---

the first job a let-down. These feelings are minimized if you have a boss who understands this frustration and exposes you to the decision-making process early in the first year. Don't become discouraged, but view your position objectively and always look to the job potential.

Decision-Making Versus Operations

It is most important to recognize that routine work is the basis of business, and therefore it must be done promptly and effectively. You cannot be promoted to upper-level management without learning the fundamentals. Since MBA graduates are often accused of wanting to be placed immediately in high management positions, you should work to dispel this myth. On the other hand, avoid making your job into that of a clerk, since it would gain you little or no respect. Never allow yourself to become totally immersed in detail. Instead, show an interest in the problem-solving area, since that is why you obtained your MBA. Be assertive and be a self-starter showing creativity and a willingness to take risks.

It is essential to achieve a delicate balance between being known as someone who is a good "nuts and bolts" operator and one who shows senior management potential. Indeed, this is the essence of your first year. During most of this period you will be working on teams as a junior, and at times your interpersonal relationships will be tested to the fullest. Sometimes it can be very frustrating working on a team, however it is absolutely essential you go through this process. It is a part of growing with the job, as you observe a team effort in action. If you try to do something alone too soon, you may produce mediocre results and be labeled accordingly. Of course, as you mature in the system, you will adopt the corporate posture, not losing your innovative and creative spirit acquired in business school.

Be sure to spend enough time working in the introductory stages of your career to avoid the temptation, as a fast-track MBA, to move too rapidly. It is much better to establish yourself as a competent, decision-making manager with a desire to learn all there is to know about each job. Even though it may be possible to move rapidly through an organization, this is usually not the best career approach in the long run. In fact, this is one of the most common complaints regarding MBAs. Being a good manager at the junior- and middle-management level is mandatory in order to understand the technical aspects of jobs that will be supervised later as a senior manager.

180

THE FIRST YEAR

Expectations

In general, the values and career-track aspirations of MBAs today differ greatly from tnose of previous years. Today's MBAs have much greater concern about values and life-styles. Also, today's MBAs are less inclined to theorize and usually want to be where the action is. There is a much greater emphasis on integrity and openness. They have a greater interest in their intellectual and emotional development. While still important, job security is less so than it was for previous MBAs, and personal growth is more important than promotions, professional recognition, and substantial incomes. Today's MBAs do not view the authority figure in the same way. They do not have the same respect for age or title but they have more respect for expertise, style, conviction, and, most important, accomplishments. MBAs today want to have greater control of their own destiny. Since most corporations do not recognize these new desires and goals, MBAs frequently encounter friction and are dissatisfied.

What should you want from your first year on the job? Generally, you want challenging, mind-stretching work. You want to be part of the decision-making process. You want to have an effect on the business. You want to be a partner to management in an open and flexible climate. You want to be emotionally involved and fulfilled. You'll generally want training programs which provide an opportunity to see a project through to the end. And while these are an MBA's expectations, most corporations are ill-equipped and not totally concerned about providing this ideal setting.

Pitfalls

At the same time MBAs articulate these desires, most sustain little drive in any one functional area. Many corporations complain that while MBAs push for growth, few stretch themselves to their limits. Yet they comment that MBAs are very bright and handle their jobs with minimum effort, and those who establish goals and discipline themselves do the best in the end.

Because MBAs are intent on themselves and their own needs, they frequently move from company to company searching for the optimal position. They frequently do not make that all-important commitment to a company, and there is also a tendency to rebel at being managed, refusing to recognize that the world is composed of hierarchies. Even if you own your own business, you are still responsible to the stockholders or to the banker. It is up to you to understand the hierarchy and work within it.

Surprisingly, despite the frequency of MBA conversation about human resources, organizational behavior, and interpersonal relationships, most MBAs do not know how to confront on a one-to-one basis. Generally, they tend to avoid interpersonal conflicts and often resist suggestions for improvement. It may take days, weeks, and even months to sell an idea to the boss; you have to have persuasion and perseverance. MBAs frequently also are impatient, exude too much confidence, and come across as critical and arrogant. This demeanor frequently threatens middle management. Be sensitive to this in dealing with supervisors.

Early Challenges and Goals

MBAs are not unworthy, but often there exists a gap between expectation and reality. MBAs come looking for challenge because they know that the more challenged they are the first year, the more successful they will be five years later. In spite of this, most companies introduce new MBAs very slowly, and they have fancy training programs which are not a challenge. Perhaps greater challenge, less training, and more pressure for high-quality work involving the profit aspects of the business would produce happier and more productive MBAs.

You can overcome any lack of challenge by creating your own challenge. Since you are used to being given projects and assignments, you perhaps do not know how to deal with an unstructured situation, a situation which can have challenging and exciting opportunities. The fast-track MBA is not passive about his or her destiny. Know how to execute your career strategy. Look for your opportunities and put your strategy into the works.

Since the first year on the job is so important in building confidence, it is important you find challenges and opportunities to use all your accumulated knowledge. This is not only important for achievement but also for self-esteem. To be psychologically successful in business, you need to be challenged, be able to set goals, and be allowed to attain the goals established. If this occurs, you will feel successful and competent and will experience a growth in self-esteem. You will become a better executive and be much more valuable to the company.

Periodically develop goals and review them with your immediate supervisor. As the training process continues, share your personal growth, frustrations, hopes, and aspirations with your supervisors. This openness contributes to a healthy relationship. As part of goal setting, establish measures of your success. What exactly do you want from this job? Review your personal and career goals now that you have that first step made.

Career Tracks

A year or two after you have learned the ropes you will start to emerge as an independent person, making and executing decisions. After having developed a reputation as a person skilled in the mechanics, you can begin working independently to produce profit for the company. You will run your own show, but this does not mean that you will be totally unsupervised or will have complete decision-making responsibility.

You will very much be in an area of specialization at this point. You can, of course, specialize in finance, sales, market research, or some other skill such as computers or statistics. You can use these skills over a wide range of company problems, but significant specialization offers the risk of losing general management mobility. Usually specialization in one or two fields is part of the foundation an MBA builds for a successful career.

You will need a specialty if for no other reason than that rank and file executives will not really respect you without it. However, since the environment changes so quickly, you cannot become expert in all fields. For the moment, be competent in one specialty to increase your confidence and become known in the company. If you have been outstanding in one area, senior management is more likely to know about you than if you are mediocre in many areas. As soon as possible, get out of the specialty mode and become a general manager. The generalist track is the path to the president's office.

After you have become accustomed to the firm and to your job, start to build lasting relationships with your peers. This will mean you will depend less on your boss and more on your mentor. It can create some problems, since some supervisors and some mentors are unwilling to "let go." This is similar to parents with college-age children; separation becomes a real problem, and for some MBAs, it is necessary to transfer to another area of the organization.

Also at this point, you should develop your own thoughts and standards while starting to exercise some creativity. Start making decisions without the approval of the boss. In doing this, you will be looking for opinions from peers and other executives outside your own immediate area.

Summary Points

How, then, should the new MBA plan his or her path to the top? The following are some general guidelines for this important process:

1. Check periodically to see if your career is progressing on schedule. Be assertive and keep pressing for your goals.

2. Learn your boss's job before you need to, but during this learning process do not make the boss competitive about the position.

3. Get known in the company. Give speeches and take seminars. Develop new concepts, work for the company's trade association, seek additional responsibilities, ask questions. Be visible.

4. Get known as a team player, making your work look good within the context of a group effort. While you should not take credit for everything, make sure you get credit for some accomplishments. If you don't toot your own horn, the horn never blows. Solo MBAs do not make it in a corporation.

5. Remain as mobile as possible. Do not move too quickly or too frequently, but leave a position or a company for a better opportunity when it comes along. Leave your old job before frustration and anger occur, or if you feel you are not on a fast track, or when your career is blocked by a boss who is not getting promoted.

6. Don't be totally consumed with your job. Maintain a private, personal life to provide the needed balance.

Appendix I

Schools That Have Accredited MBA Programs

Member	Year of Initial Membership	Dean
University of Akron	1966	James W. Dunlap
University of Alabama	1929	John S. Fielden
University of Alabama in Birmingham	1973	N. Gene Newport
University of Alberta	1968	R. S. Smith
University of Arizona	1948	William Barrett
Arizona State University	1962	Glenn D. Overman
University of Arkansas	1931	John P. Owen
Atlanta University	1974	A. H. Sterne
Baylor University	1950	Richard C. Scott
Boston College	1956	John J. Neuhauser
Boston University	1921	Jules J. Schwartz
Bowling Green University	1954	Karl E. Vogt
Brigham Young University	1963	William G. Dyer
University of California	1916	Earl F. Cheit
University of California, Los Angeles	1939	J. Clayburn LaForce, Jr.
California State University, Chico	1972	Frederick M. Whipple
California State University, Fresno	1959	Gene R. Burton
California State University, Fullerton	1965	Henry R. Anderson
California State University, Long Beach	1971	Seymour Marshak
California State University, Los Angeles	1960	Donald G. Malcolm
California State University, Sacramento	1963	Austin J. Gerber
Carnegie-Mellon University	1957	Robert S. Kaplan
Case Western Reserve University	1958	Theodore M. Alfred
University of Central Florida	1975	Clifford L. Eubanks

SCHOOLS THAT HAVE ACCREDITED MBA PROGRAMS

Member	Year of Initial Membership	Dean
University of Chicago	1916	Richard N. Rosett
University of Cincinnati	1919	Albert J. Simone
Cleveland State University	1974	Ephraim P. Smith
University of Colorado	1938	William H. Baughn
Colorado State University	1970	D. W. Dobler
Columbia University	1916	Boris Yavitz
University of Connecticut	1958	Ronald J. Patten
Cornell University	1950	David A. Thomas
Dartmouth College	1916	Richard R. West
University of Denver	1923	Ronald R. Gist
DePaul University	1957	James A. Hart
University of Detroit	1949	Sam Barone
Drake University	1949	Richard G. Peebler
Drexel University	1967	Paul E. Dascher
Duke University	1979	Thomas F. Keller
Duquesne University	1961	Blair J. Kolasa
East Carolina University	1967	James H. Bearden
Emory University	1949	George M. Parks
University of Florida	1929	Robert F. Lanzillotti
Florida Atlantic University	1977	Gary L. Luing
University of Georgia	1926	William C. Flewellen, Jr
Georgia Institute of Technology	1969	Charles Gearing
Georgia State University	1960	Kenneth Black, Jr.
Harvard University	1916	John McArthur
University of Hawaii	1967	David A. Heenan
University of Houston	1964	A. Benton Cocanougher
University of Illinois at Urbana-Champaign	1924	V. K. Zimmerman
Indiana University	1921	Schuyler F. Ottesen
University of Iowa	1923	J. Richard Zecher
University of Kansas	1925	Joseph A. Pichler
Kent State University	1964	Stanley Hille
University of Kentucky	1926	W. W. Ecton
Lehigh University	1938	Richard W. Barsness
Louisiana State University	1931	Don L. Woodland
Louisiana Tech University	1955	Bob R. Owens
Loyola University (New Orleans)	1950	Joseph M. Bonin
Marquette University	1928	Thomas A. Bausch
University of Maryland	1940	Rudolph A. Lamone
University of Massachusetts	1958	Harry T. Allen

APPENDIX I

Member	Year of Initial Membership	Dean
Massachusetts Institute of Technology	1957	William F. Pounds
Memphis State University	1970	M. E. Bond
University of Miami	1957	Edward J. Fox
Miami University	1932	Bill R. Moeckel
University of Michigan	1919	Gilbert R. Whitaker
Michigan State University	1953	Richard J. Lewis
University of Minnesota	1920	David M. Lilly
University of Mississippi	1944	Carl W. Nabors
Mississippi State University	1960	Gaines M. Rogers
University of Missouri-Columbia	1926	S. Watson Dunn
University of Missouri-Kansas City	1969	Jack D. Heysinger
University of Missouri-St. Louis	1970	Donald H. Driemeier
University of Nebraska-Lincoln	1916	Gary Schwendiman
University of Nevada-Reno	1961	Richard H. Hughs
University of New Mexico	1975	William S. Peters
University of New Orleans	1969	John E. Altazan
University of North Carolina at Chapel Hill	1923	John P. Evans
North Texas State University	1961	Marvin H. Berkeley
Northeast Louisiana University	1972	Van Cook McGraw
Northeastern University	1962	Philip McDonald
Northern Arizona University	1969	Frank H. Besnette
Northern Illinois University	1969	James D. Benson
Northwestern University	1961	Donald P. Jacobs
University of Notre Dame	1962	Leo V. Ryan, CSV
Ohio State University	1916	H. Justin Davidson
Ohio University	1950	Gerald Silver
University of Oklahoma	1926	Lawrence E. McKibbin
Oklahoma State University	1958	Robert L. Sandmeyer
University of Oregon	1923	James E. Reinmuth
Oregon State University	1960	Earl Goddard
Pacific Lutheran University	1971	Gundar J. King
University of Pennsylvania	1916	Donald C. Carroll
Pennsylvania State University	1957	Eugene J. Kelley
University of Pittsburgh	1916	H. J. Zoffer
Purdue University	1967	Keith R. Smith
University of Rhode Island	1969	Richard R. Weeks
University of Rochester	1964	William H. Meckling
Rutgers-The State University of New Jersey	1941	Horace J. DePodwin
Saint Louis University	1948	John Wagner

SCHOOLS THAT HAVE ACCREDITED MBA PROGRAMS

Member	Year of Initial Membership	Dean
San Diego State University	1959	Allan R. Bailey
San Francisco State University	1963	Arthur F. Cunningham
San Jose State University	1967	George C. Halverson
University of Santa Clara	1953	Andre L. Delbecq
University of South Carolina	1962	James F. Kane
University of South Dakota	1949	Dale E. Clement
University of Southern California	1922	Jack D. Steele
Southern Illinois University at Carbondale	1962	John R. Darling
Southern Methodist University	1925	Alan B. Coleman
Stanford University	1926	Robert K. Jaedicke
State University of New York at Albany	1974	William K. Holstein
State University of New York at Buffalo	1930	Joseph A. Alutto
Syracuse University	1920	L. Richard Oliker
Temple University	1934	Edward M. Mazze
University of Tennessee, Knoxville	1941	C. Warren Neel
University of Texas at Arlington	1969	W. E. Mullendore
University of Texas at Austin	1916	George Kosmetsky
Texas A&M University	1972	William V. Muse
Texas Christian University	1963	Edward A. Johnson
The University of Toledo	1955	Edward Bardi
Tulane University	1916	Walter O. Spencer
University of Tulsa	1949	Clifford E. Hutton
University of Utah	1936	Blaine Huntsman
Vanderbilt University	1979	Samuel B. Richmond
University of Virginia	1925	C. Stewart Sheppard
Virginia Polytechnic Institute and State University	1966	H. H. Mitchell
University of Washington	1921	Kermit O. Hanson
Washington State University	1950	Gary Walton
Washington University	1921	Robert L. Virgil
West Virginia University	1954	Jack L. Turner
Wichita State University	1968	Douglas Sharp
College of William and Mary	1972	Charles L. Quittmeyer
University of Wisconsin-Madison	1916	Robert H. Bock
University of Wisconsin-Milwaukee	1970	Eric Schenker
University of Wisconsin-Oshkosh	1970	Clifford E. Larson

SOURCE: American Assembly of Collegiate Schools of Business Membership Directory 1979–80

Appendix II

Employment Agencies in Selected Major Metropolitan Areas

ATLANTA

AAA Employment
1 Perimeter Way; 955-7756

Abernathy Personnel Consultants
3379 Peachtree Road; 261-2277

Accountants Unlimited
230 Peachtree Street; 688-6252

Accountemps
3379 Peachtree Road; 266-2153

Alan Associates Personnel Center
1 Perimeter Way; 952-0758

Argo Quest
180 Allen Road; 255-5118

Arnold Personnel Services, Inc.
150 Interstate North Parkway; 955-5056

Associated Business Careers
180 Allen Road; 257-0001

Atlanta Arts Agency
3384 Peachtree Road; 266-8180

Atlanta Management Analysis Systems, Inc.
3480 Greenbriar Parkway; 344-1777

Atlanta Recruiting Corporation
1925 Century Boulevard; 633-4173

Bal Ltd.
Cain Tower; 581-0040

Baker & Associates
450 Harris Tower; 266-8413

Baste Personnel
229 Peachtree Street; 588-0666

Bell Oaks Personnel
3400 Peachtree Road; 261-2170

Bob Maddox Associates
3390 Peachtree Road; 231-0558

Browne Information Systems
229 Peachtree Street; 523-0500

Burden, Sara
1815 Century Boulevard; 636-5000

Business Men's Clearing House
225 Peachtree Street; 681-3810

Career Associates, Inc.
5780 Peachtree Road; 256-4242

Career Concepts
3272 Peachtree Road; 231-5901

Career Consultant, Inc.
2801 Buford Highway; 321-5901

Career Development Corporation
100 Colony Square; 892-0992

Career Recruiters
245 W Wieuca Road; 252-9175

Career Services, Inc.
1819 Peachtree Road; 355-7365

Careers of Atlanta, Inc.
4400 Ashford Road; 396-7707

Clark Associates-Industrial
1800 Century Boulevard; 321-3037

Colony Office Mates
400 Colony Square; 892-1900

Computer Source
305 River Knoll Drive; 394-2032

Construction Careers
3301 Buckeye Road; 458-0515

Corporate Personnel, Inc.
4651 Roswell Road; 252-3292

Cosmopolitan Personnel Systems, Inc.
3400 Peachtree Road; 237-7680

Cyberway
229 Peachtree Street; 523-0500

Duke Personnel, Inc.
3312 Piedmont Road; 237-2111

Dunhill of Atlanta, Inc.
3445 Peachtree Road; 261-3751

EDP Search, Inc.
3355 Lenox Road; 262-1210

Engineering Careers
3301 Buckeye Road; 458-0515

Execu-Resources
1800 Century Boulevard; 325-7767

Executive Recruiters, Inc.
2895 Whitby Drive; 491-3001

Flair Personnel
Lenox Towers; 231-0101

Fortune Personnel Agency
3400 Peachtree Road; 231-2253

Fox & Associates
233 Peachtree Street; 659-4141

Fox-Morris Associates, Inc.
47 Perimeter Center; 393-0933

George & Associates
76 E Perimeter Center; 396-3895

King Personnel Consultants
3390 Peachtree Road; 266-1800

Lendman Associates
1945 The Exchange; 952-0822

Lucas Associates
3379 Peachtree Road; 266-2772

Management Personnel Services
3525 Piedmont Road; 231-2007

Management Search, Inc.
Peachtree Center, Harris Tower; 659-5050

Manning & Associates Personnel, Inc.
233 Peachtree Street; 577-5003

Mengert & Associates
485 Tara Tower; 255-8025

Metropolitan Personnel, Inc.
3379 Peachtree Road; 261-8666

Mills Management, Inc.
2600 Century Parkway; 325-0555

Mitchell Kot Personnel Services, Inc.
225 Peachtree Street; 577-5080

National Computer Associates
Cain Tower; 581-0040

Nazal Employment Service
2158 Cascade Road; 753-4433

Niemann Personnel Service
3390 Peachtree Road; 262-2760

Noble & Anglin, Inc.
2300 Henderson Mill Road; 491-0056

Norrell Services, Inc.
300 Wendell Court; 696-4121

Northside Personnel Consultants
47 Perimeter Center; 393-1613

O'Keefe Personnel Services
3384 Peachtree Road; 266-1153

Olsten Permanent Personnel
229 Peachtree Street; 699-6115

Omni Search
1925 Century Boulevard; 325-3363

Opportunities Unlimited, Inc.
229 Peachtree Street; 681-3440

Pace Associates
5775 Peachtree Road; 255-4868

Paces Personnel Services, Inc.
Peachtree Center South; 688-5307

Paden & Associates
Standard Federal Savings Building; 525-0926

Pair Personnel Service
2964 Peachtree Road; 261-3566

Parker Dow & Associates
4651 Roswell Road; 252-9980

Parnassus Personnel Consultants
133 Luckie Street; 525-6895

Pascoe Enterprises-Electronics
1330 University Drive; 892-2636

Pathfinders Personnel, Inc.
235 Peachtree Street; 688-5940

Perimeter Placement
245 W Perimeter Center; 393-0000

Personnel Enterprises
3390 Peachtree Road; 261-1926

Personnel Opportunities, Inc.
3390 Peachtree Road; 261-0702

Personnel Pool of America
100 Wendell Court; 696-1444

Pettway & Co.
3565 Piedmont Road; 231-0000

**Premier Personnel-Division
Lucas Associates, Inc.**
3379 Peachtree Road; 266-8911

Professional Employment Consultants
2675 Cumberland Parkway; 434-7198

Professional Insurance Careers, Inc.
3301 Buckeye Road; 452-1190

Quest Systems, Inc.
11 Corporate Boulevard; 636-3000

Renvan Personnel
2970 Peachtree Road; 262-2422

Retail Personnel Search
2220 Parklake Drive; 491-1199

Retail Recruiters, Inc.
3400 Peachtree Road; 231-9444

Robco Associates, Inc.
2840 Mount Wilkinson Parkway; 435-6700

Romac and Associates
3340 Peachtree Road; 231-3535

Ross Scott Associates
2220 Parklake Drive; 493-7070

Roth Young of Atlanta
235 Peachtree Street; 577-5970

Sales Careers
3301 Buckeye Road; 458-0515

Sales Opportunities Unlimited, Inc.
5600 Roswell Road; 256-9314

Salesforce
3400 Peachtree Road; 262-3155

Sanford Rose Associates
134 Peachtree Street; 524-6094

Scroggins Personnel Consultants
5600 Roswell Road; 256-5545

Search Consultants
2200 Parklake Drive; 939-9800

Smith Associates
3400 Peachtree Road; 266-1022

**Snelling & Snelling
Personnel Consultants**
3355 Lenox Road; 262-7111

Solomon Associates
2220 Parklake Drive; 491-1199

Southeastern Associates, Inc.
3390 Peachtree Road; 231-8515

Spectrum Personnel Consultants
3400 Peachtree Road; 231-9444

Thompson Consultants, Inc.
3390 Peachtree Road; 261-4593

Tops Personnel Service, Inc.
100 Colony Square; 892-1723

Washington Employment Bureau
51 Elliott Street; 524-1803

Wells Recruiting Systems
2200 Century Parkway; 321-5425

Whitlow & Associates
3390 Peachtree Road; 262-2566

Whittaker & Associates
2675 Cumberland Parkway; 434-3779

BOSTON

Accounting Register
333 Federal Street; 482-2800

Active Personnel Consultants
100 Boylston Street; 426-0007

Administrative Resources, Inc.
739 Boylston Street; 266-5010

Affiliated Associates
1730 Beacon Street; 738-0344

American Nurse, Inc.
210 Lincoln Street; 451-0295

American Personnel
535 Boylston Street; 266-4200

Andrews Associates
189 State Street; 720-4600

BPC, Inc.
729 Boylston Street; 536-1991

Banker's Search of Boston, Inc.
60 State Street; 523-4570

Barclay Personnel Systems
500 Boylston Street; 262-2660

Boston Executive Recruitment Consultants
729 Boylston Street; 536-1991

Bostonian Personnel
6 Faneuil Hall Market Place; 367-8771

Breen Data
50 Milk Street; 266-7129

Burr Inc.
18 Tremont Street; 723-2040

Burton Personnel Service
120 Boylston Street; 482-1950

Business Men's Clearing House
545 Boylston Street; 267-9119

Cain & Associates
60 State Street; 367-9540

Career House
41 Winter Street; 426-5660

Circle Employment
60 State Street; 367-2600

Cleary Consultants
89 State Street; 367-7189

Compusearch
607 Boylston Street; 262-5054

Contemporaries of Boston Inc.
8 Winter Street; 426-5682

Data Positions
1 McKinley Square; 367-9200

Diamond Personnel Consultants
15 Court Square; 742-5700

Dumont Kiradjieff & Moriarty
79 Milk Street; 451-9212

Dunhill of Boston, Inc.
5 Faneuil Hall Market Place; 227-4620

Engineers Index
133 Federal Street; 482-2800

Executive Sources International
66 Long Wharf; 523-2525

Fairfield Whitney, Inc.
21 Merchants Row; 367-0022

Forasco
73 Tremont Street; 367-5088

Haldane Associates
545 Boylston Street; 437-7110

Hardy-Dana-Insurance Personnel
65 Franklin Street; 357-5380

Harrington Associates
148 State Street; 227-1626

Health Care Professionals, Inc.
73 Tremont Street; 742-2772

Hire Agency
101 Tremont Street; 426-5511

Hotel & Restaurant Personnel of America, Inc.
184 High Street; 367-6755

Insurance Careers, Inc.
66 Long Wharf; 367-0336

Insurance Recruiters
101 Tremont Street; 357-8243

Insurance Resource Group
Faneuil Hall Market Place; 367-6722

JNB Associates
75 Federal Street; 451-0355

Johnson Associates, Inc.
10 Post Office Square; 227-2337

Koteen Associates
50 Milk Street; 482-0066

L & L Associates
73 Tremont Street; 227-4130

Leonard Personnel Associates, Inc.
60 State Street; 523-8311

Management Recruiters
607 Boylston Street; 262-5050

McCusker Associates
Faneuil Hall Market Place; 367-5954

OPA Personnel Consultants
2 Center Plaza; 523-5155

Personnel Resources Group, Inc.
44 School Street; 227-3333

Personnel Systems International, Inc.
133 Federal Street; 482-2800

Pilgrim Personnel
120 Boylston Street; 482-9732

Positions, Inc.
1 McKinley Square; 367-9200

Prime Positions
335 Boylston Street; 244-5100

Professional Placement Associates
960A Park Square Building; 426-2080

Promotions Co.
1 Center Plaza; 227-7722

R & D Associates
755 Boylston Street; 262-0870

Retail Register
133 Federal Street; 482-2800

Robert Half of Boston, Inc.
100 Summer Street; 423-1200

Rogers & Sands, Inc.
100 Federal Street; 426-4180

Romac & Associates
125 High Street; 482-6616

Roth Young Personnel Service
177 Milk Street; 482-7377

Russillo's
60 State Street; 720-1113

Scott-Wayne Associates
545 Boylston Street; 267-6505

Selected Executives, Inc.
959 Park Square Building; 426-3100

Source Personnel
175 Federal Street; 482-7613

Trans World Overseas Employment Services
10 Tremont Street; 723-7875

Trans World Recruitment Specialists
10 Tremont Street; 723-7874

Transitional Employment Enterprises, Inc.
184 High Street; 482-7430

Universal Management Associates
6 Faneuil Hall Market Place; 367-1110

Ward & Associates, Inc.
1041 Park Square Building; 482-4959

Webster Personnel, Inc.
1 Court Street; 742-2030

Windsor Greene Associates
545 Boylston Street; 267-6505

CHICAGO

ABC Personnel
400 E. Randolph Street; 527-1291

Abbott Personnel
8 S. Michigan Avenue; 580-0003

Accountants Center, Ltd.
7 W. Madison Street; 782-3960

Accurate Personnel
9 S. Fairview Park Ridge; 693-4907

Action Personnel
180 W. Washington Street; 641-1240

Ad World Personnel
333 N. Michigan Street; 726-7691

Admiral Employment Bureau, Inc.
11 E. Adam Street; 922-0685

Advocate Employment Service
3402 N. Ashland Street; 975-7800

Amdo Accountants
55 E. Monroe Street; 726-4591

American Personnel Consultants, Inc.
30 W. Washington Street; 263-6463

Analitis, Jim
30 W. Washington Street; 236-3951

Andy Garrigan Personnel
53 W. Jackson Street; 427-1545

B J Placement Center
5715 N. Ashland Street; 989-7294

Bankers Associates, Inc.
22 W. Monroe Street; 263-1063

Bankers Group
120 S. Riverside Plaza; 930-1111

Bankers Personnel Service
11 S. LaSalle Street; 332-7190

Bassler & Associates
343 S. Dearborn Street; 427-6579

Belson Hemingway & Associates
327 S. LaSalle Street; 939-6210

Beris Employment Agency
4962 N. Milwaukee Street; 736-9448

EMPLOYMENT AGENCIES IN SELECTED MAJOR METROPOLITAN AREAS

Bette Pauls Careers
500 N. Michigan Avenue; 822-0506

Boston Personnel Consultants
100 N. LaSalle Street; 853-3630

Brewster Associates
444 N. Michigan Avenue; 642-6000

Breyer Personnel
135 S. LaSalle Street; 236-7180

Britt Associates, Inc.
53 W. Jackson Street; 427-9450

Bryant Associates, Inc.
875 N. Michigan Avenue; 649-0700

Business & Professional Office Services, Inc.
10 S. LaSalle Street; 372-4393

Business Management Personnel
150 S. Wacker Drive; 782-6062

C F F & Associates, Inc.
9400 W. Foster Road; 992-2382

Cadillac Associates, Inc.
32 W. Randolph Street; 346-9400

Canyon & Associates
25 E. Washington Street; 332-2288

Careers Unlimited
360 N. Michigan Avenue; 227-3377

Casey Services, Inc.
333 E. Ontario Street; 649-0755

Central Clearing, Inc.
7034 W. North Street; 637-2700

Chester Employment Centers
17313 Oak Park Avenue; 568-7080

Chicago Personnel Service
5935 S. Pulaski Street; 581-1774

Clark, Ken
14 E. Jackson Boulevard; 663-0770

Co-op Recruiting Systems
7 W. Madison Avenue; 726-1927

Coleman Registry
10907 S. Wabash Street; 928-3938

Compupro
55 W. Monroe Street; 263-5507

Computer Providers, Inc.
55 W. Monroe Street; 263-5507

Computer Services
180 N. Michigan Avenue; 641-0490

Concept Corp.
625 N. Michigan Avenue; 280-1717

Cooley-Baker, Inc.
111 E. Wacker Drive; 467-4444

Cornell Employment
4070 S. Archer Street; 376-8620

Daneen Associates
505 N. Lake Street; 828-9843

Data Base Consultants
55 E. Jackson Street; 322-1400

Data Career Center
Prudential Plaza; 565-1060

Datapath 2000, Inc.
6170 N. Lemont Street; 725-1505

Designed Careers, Inc.
180 N. LaSalle Street; 236-5373

Dunhill of Chicago, Inc.
230 N. Michigan Avenue; 346-0933

Employers Services Bureau
209 W. Jackson Street; 987-2666

Engineering Agency
150 S. Wacker Drive; 977-4800

Engineering Consultants, Co.
2441 N. Laramie Street; 889-6620

Esquire Personnel Service, Inc.
180 N. Michigan Avenue; 346-6800

Euro Employment & Maintenance, Inc.
2858 N. Milwaukee Avenue; 235-0300

EVC International Placement Agency
400 E. Randolph Street; 337-6010

Execupower, Inc.
11 S. LaSalle Street; 332-5795

Executive Suite Personnel
625 N. Michigan Avenue; 266-6601

Fardig Associates
176 W. Adams Street; 332-1480

Ferry Associates
176 W. Adams Street; 443-1160

Field Engineering Enterprises
360 N. Michigan Avenue; 726-1666

First Personnel North, Inc.
4872 N. Milwaukee Street; 286-2636

Fortune Personnel Consultants
55 E. Jackson Street; 461-9640

Fortune Personnel of Chicago
500 N. Michigan Avenue; 467-9130

Fox Services, Inc.
173 W. Madison Street; 372-0914

Fulline Systems, Inc.
180 N. Michigan Avenue; 641-1729

Garrigan Personnel
53 W. Jackson Street; 427-1545

General Employment Enterprises
150 S. Wacker Drive; 977-9300

Godfrey Personnel, Inc.
209 LaSalle Street; 236-4455

Gomez & Associates
120 W. Madison Avenue; 346-5525

Green Guaranty Company
7 W. Madison Avenue; 372-5800

Hirtz & Associates, Inc.
150 N. Wacker Drive; 977-1555

Hunt Personnel of Chicago
5725 E. River Road; 693-4401

Hurley & Associates, Inc.
200 W. Monroe Street; 782-6288

Inroads, Inc.
407 S. Dearborn Avenue; 663-9892

Institute for Management & Resource Development
1 E. Wacker Drive; 467-1111

International Recruiters, Inc.
624 S. Michigan Avenue; 939-0013

Interviewing Consultants, Inc.
25 E. Washington Street; 263-1710

Interviewing Dynamics
444 N. Michigan Avenue; 836-1200

Ivy Personnel, Inc.
4770 N. Lincoln Street; 275-0400

J. & J. Recruitment Service, Ltd.
179 W. Washington Street; 236-7818

J. R. Chicago Personnel Service
5935 S. Pulaski Street; 581-1774

Jackson Employment Agency
207 S. Wabash Avenue; 427-7320

Jacobson Associates
221 N. LaSalle Street; 726-1578

Keith Ross & Associates, Inc.
150 N. Wacker Drive; 558-1850

Kellum Employment Agency
19 W. Jackson Boulevard; 939-8100

Kennedy Group Inc.
150 W. Wacker Drive; 372-0099

Key Personnel Services
4006 N. Milwaukee Avenue; 777-0661

Kingsley Employment Service
208 S. LaSalle Street; 726-8190

Klatt Employment Services, Inc.
105 W. Madison Avenue; 263-5737

Landmark Personnel Services, Inc.
179 W. Washington Street; 853-0123

Landry Personnel
11 S. LaSalle Street; 346-4760

Lendman Associates, Ltd.
875 N. Michigan Avenue; 337-4300

Life Personnel Services
14 E. Jackson Boulevard; 332-3885

Lincoln Management Services
5 S. Wabash Street; 641-1974

Lockman Associates, Inc.
100 N. LaSalle Street; 855-1100

M B A Registry
300 S. Wacker Drive; 341-9051

M. W. Search, Inc.
29 E. Madison Avenue; 781-0070

Maharlika Employment Service, Inc.
30 N. Michigan Avenue; 641-3343

Management Information Personnel, Inc.
333 N. Michigan Avenue; 346-3904

Management Recruiters
173 W. Madison Street; 648-1800

Management Resources, Inc.
30 N. LaSalle Street; 977-1300

Marshall Associates
5903 N. Caldwell Road; 736-6536

Masters Associates
200 W. Monroe Street; 332-0444

McCoy & Associates, Inc.
55 E. Washington Street; 726-3221

Metro Search, Inc.
79 W. Monroe Street; 782-6804

Meyers & Associates
500 N. Michigan Avenue; 751-1027

Mid America Consultants
333 N. Michigan Avenue; 580-0160

Modern Employment Service, Inc.
7 W. Madison Avenue; 782-3960

Monarch Systems, Inc.
333 N. Michigan Avenue; 782-1200

Nadler Group Incorporated
120 W. Madison Avenue; 621-0020

O'Meara Associates
166 E. Superior; 337-6211

O'Shea Employment System
64 E. Jackson Avenue; 987-2669

Opportunity Personnel Service
220 S. State Street; 427-7874

PMA Employment Specialists, Inc.
180 N. Michigan Avenue; 236-9036

Pahlman, Murphy & Attridge
180 N. Michigan Avenue; 236-9036

Personnel Group
Prudential Plaza; 565-1770

Personnel Management Services
4753 N. Broadway; 878-3038

Pioneer Personnel, Inc.
36 S. Wabash Street; 346-7075

Plaza, Inc.
55 E. Monroe Street; 263-0944

Pointer & Associates
173 W. Madison Avenue; 782-4374

Polbrat Employment Agency
1645 N. Damen Street; 772-2521

Professional Employment Services, Inc.
189 W. Madison Avenue; 346-4300

Profile Personnel, Inc.
36 S. Wabash Street; 641-0540

Rac Personnel Service
5412 N. Clark Street; 334-3010

R&G Personnel Service
53 W. Jackson Boulevard; 922-9577

Ramco Personnel Resources
228 S. Wabash Avenue; 461-9632

Regency Personnel
520 N. Michigan Avenue; 944-6929

Reliable Personnel
3204 N. Central Street; 725-8000

Robert Half of Chicago, Inc.
35 E. Wacker Drive; 782-6930

Roland Greyhound Employment Agency
30 N. Michigan Avenue; 781-7200

Sales & Management Search, Inc.
120 S. Riverside Plaza; 930-1111

Sanford Rose Associates
189 W. Madison Avenue; 236-0958

Schield Personnel
55 E. Washington Street; 782-7884

Select Personnel, Inc.
14 E. Jackson Street; 922-7737

Source EDP, Inc.
100 S. Wacker Drive; 782-0857

Star Personnel Corp.
333 N. Michigan Avenue; 726-6100

Synergetics
343 S. Dearborn Street; 663-1124

Thomas & Associates, Inc.
2315 E. 103rd Street; 731-7800

Trempe & Associates
55 W. Monroe Street; 236-7301

Tri Associates, Inc.
624 S. Michigan Avenue; 663-1851

Tri-Continental Personnel
63 E. Adams Street; 663-6000

VIP Personnel Center
5151 N. Harlem Avenue; 774-7313

Vance Personnel
149 W. Chicago Avenue; 787-1181

Wabash Employment Agency
202 S. State Street; 922-5020

West Personnel Service
28 Yorktown Street; 627-7400

Wood Computer Associates, Inc.
79 W. Monroe Street; 368-0633

Word Pros Personnel
5 S. Wabash Avenue; 372-6175

Worldwide Employment Systems
1020 S. Wabash Avenue; 922-3843

York Employment Services
190 N. State Street; 782-2075

DALLAS

A-Dal East Personnel Service
12-10 Old Gate Road; 328-9101

AMH Placement Service
14800 Quorum Drive; 661-9558

Accent Placement Service
300 Bishop Avenue; 644-6908

Account Abilities Personnel Services
5520 L B J Freeway; 980-4184

Accounting Personnel Consultants
14114 Dallas Parkway; 386-4770

Act I Personnel
6300 N. Central Expressway; 739-5843

Action EDP
2808 Oak Lawn; 368-6416

Action Employment Service
1536 S. Center Street; 261-7591

Advanced Personnel
2814 Elm Street; 263-1447

Allan Personnel Service
9106 Garland Road; 328-8403

Allied Personnel Service
6220 Gaston Avenue; 827-9191

American Employment Agency
835 N. Hampton Road; 223-6711

Anchor Personnel Consultants
725 S. Central Expressway; 669-3216

Ann Rowe Employment Service
3409 Oak Lawn; 521-5822

Answer Personnel Services
5510 Abrams; 692-9236

B. P. and Associates
2930 Turtle Creek Plaza; 521-7970

Babich & Associates, Inc.
2001 Bryan Tower; 741-3891

Bent Tree Personnel Services
16475 Dallas Parkway; 931-2325

Birnbach & Associates, Inc.
6750 Hillcrest Plaza Drive; 386-7901

Bob White Associates
6060 N. Central Expressway; 750-7348

Britt-Alert Personnel Services
Midway Bank Building; 264-4241

Brooks Brownsted & Associates
5757 Alpha Road; 387-3300

Brown & Keene Personnel Consultants, Inc.
350 N. St. Paul Street; 651-8960

Bundy-Stewart Associates, Inc.
12800 Hillcrest Road; 458-0626

Burnett's Employment Services, Inc.
2710 Avenue E; 261-4411

Business Men's Clearing House
8300 Douglas Street; 363-7370

Business World Employment Consultants
4030 Lemmon Street; 522-3890

Butler Knox, Inc.
5944 Luther Lane; 373-0088

Byrd International, Inc.
1111 W. Mockingbird Lane; 630-4000

C A Personnel, Inc.
6350 L B J Freeway; 458-1470

Capital Personnel Service
Capital Bank Building; 826-0750

Capticorn Career Consultants
3300 W. Mockingbird Lane; 353-0202

Career Brokers
2818 Country Club; 278-4701

Career Sales, Inc.
1010 W. Mockingbord Lane; 630-5311

Career Search Consultants, Inc.
14800 Quorum Drive; 385-0808

Career Woman Personnel
1525 Elm Street; 744-0053

Career Unlimited Personnel Service, Inc.
11300 N. Central Expressway; 750-9913

Carrie & Company Placement Service
1309 Main Street; 741-4196

Carter & Associates, Inc.
First Bank & Trust Building; 234-3296

Celia Inc. of Dallas
9550 Forest Lane; 343-1110

Central Professional Services
13773 N. Central Expressway; 699-3865

Charlotte Donnelly Personnel Consultants
440 Northlake Shopping Center; 349-9048

Clark Employment Service
8609 Northwest Plaza Drive; 363-8383

Cobb Associates
2560 Royal Lane; 243-0391

Cockrell Hull Employment Service, Inc.
Valley View Bank Building; 387-0206

Computer Careers
4101 McEwen; 387-4010

Computer Centre
8350 N. Central Expressway; 987-0762

Computer Recruiting Consultants
2925 L B J Freeway; 243-7791

Contax Career Consultants
14580 E. Beltwood Parkway; 458-1202

Continental Personnel Service
701 N. Central Expressway; 699-1925

Cooksey Associates
12700 Preston Road; 386-7272

Cope, Inc.
400 A Lancaster; 371-0090

Corporate Personnel Consultants, Inc.
8333 Douglas; 363-1800

Corporate Staff Recruiters
4455 L B J Freeway; 233-9436

Craig Affiliates Personnel Consultants, Inc.
7616 L B J Freeway; 980-1544

Crenshaw & Associates
10551 Black Walnut; 234-8726

Crowe Personnel
3003 L B J Freeway; 484-3003

Crown Agency
3003 L B J Freeway; 247-4994

DFW Personnel Service
1327-A Brown Tower; 268-6923

DPCareer Improvements, Inc.
14114 Dallas Parkway; 783-1385

Dallas Employment Service
1507 Pacific Avenue; 742-5741

Dallas North Employment Agency
8350 N. Central Expressway; 369-8332

Damon & Associates
7515 Greenville Avenue; 696-6990

Daniel Associates Personnel Consultants
7100 Grapevine Highway; 589-7237

Data Resources, Inc.
2974 L B J Freeway; 241-8595

Datapro Personnel Consultants
5580 L B J Freeway; 661-8600

Davidson & Associates
1949 Stemmons Freeway; 749-0100

Davisson-Newport Associates
600 S. Central Expressway; 690-9621

DeAnn White Personnel
11332 Mathis Avenue; 484-3328

Design Personnel Consultants
6060 N. Central Expressway; 739-5143

Direction Data Personnel Consultants
11311 N. Central Expressway; 361-9303

Diversified Human Resources Group
14001 Goldmark; 783-1006

Diversified Management Clearing House
5501 L B J Freeway; 960-0331

Donnelly Personnel Consultants
440 Northlake Shopping Center; 349-9048

Duncanville Employment Agency
431 W. Wheatland; 298-2900

Dunhill of Dallas, Inc.
13101 Preston Road; 661-9494

ESP Personnel Service
6350 L B J Freeway; 385-0453

Eden Management Personnel
1324 Summerwood; 661-0306

Employers Group
2829 W. Northwest Highway; 351-2882

Employment Personnel Consultants, Inc.
9221 L B J Freeway; 669-1434

Employment Resources
915 S. Hampton Road; 942-4450

Employment Search & Placement
14800 Quorum Drive; 934-8067

Employment Systems, Inc.
7701 Stemmons Freeway; 638-8776

Equinox Personnel Consultants
10884 Harry Hines; 358-3521

Evins Personnel Consultants
2108 E. Randol Mill Road; 261-1161

Executive Recruiters International
6620 Northwood Road; 373-6125

Executive Resources Search Consultants
8350 Meadow Road; 361-8972

Financial & Accounting Search Bureau
Centre Tower; 980-4090

Fidelity Employment Agency
Fidelity Building; 747-6074

First Place Personnel Consultants
One Main Place; 748-9004

Foust Employment Consultant
305 Loop 820; 589-7318

Goldberg & Associates
2828 Forest Lane; 241-4075

Gould-Massey Personnel Services
211 N. Ervay Building; 747-7771

Gragg Personnel Service
13999 Goldmark; 234-5007

Graham & Associates, Inc.
13601 Preston Road; 980-1998

Greater Dallas Personnel Consultants
8350 N. Central Expressway; 987-0276

Grove Employment, Inc.
6434 E. Mockingbird Lane; 826-9060

HLM & Associates
6200 Maple Avenue; 350-6404

Hollenshead & Associates, Inc.
8150 N. Central Expressway; 691-2140

Innes Associates
Stemmons Tower West; 630-8351

Innovators Personnel Consultants
4115 N. Central Expressway; 522-9210

**Insurance Personnel Placement
  Associates, Inc.**
One Northpark East; 696-0663

**Insurance Recruiters Personnel
  Consultants**
3707 Rawlins; 528-0090

International Personnel Agency, Inc.
1901 Central Drive; 267-2661

International Search
1200 Main Street; 741-7372

J & D Personnel Recruiters
725 Lamar Boulevard East; 265-4715

Jackson Employment Agency
211 N. Erway Street; 741-5948

Jacobson Associates
8350 N. Central Expressway; 739-0775

**James & Associates Personnel
  Consultants**
2964 L B J Freeway; 241-5100

Jean West Associates, Inc.
1341 W. Mockingbird Lane; 630-8411

Key Personnel
First Bank & Trust Building; 235-8371

Kirkland Personnel Services
8585 Stemmons Freeway; 630-2790

LeMiles and Company
8563 Manderville Avenue; 750-5800

Lendman Associates Southwest
1600 Promenade Street; 783-8800

Lineback Associates
Campbell Centre; 750-7250

Lucas Associates, Inc.
8700 Stemmons Freeway; 634-1650

MLO, Inc.
3635 Noble; 526-4621

Management Personnel Search
6060 N. Central Expressway; 368-5188

Management Personnel Services
1341 W. Mockingbird Lane; 688-0330

Martin Harris And Associates, Inc.
7515 Greenville Avenue; 691-3430

Martin Henderson & Associates, Inc.
12700 Park Central Drive; 233-3112

Martin Personnel
7839 Churchill Way; 386-7904

Metro Recruiters
2925 L B J Freeway; 241-9084

**Metroplex Association of Personnel
  Consultants**
211 N. Ervay; 742-6733

Metroplex Personnel Services
7001 Grapevine Highway; 589-7321

Midway Personnel Service
818-A E. Abram Street; 261-0781

Miller Personnel Services, Inc.
333 W. Campbell Road; 231-5306

Miller Personnel Consultants
8333 Douglas; 361-0080

Minority Search, Inc.
777 Thornton; 948-6116

Minority Women Employment Program
109 N. Akard Street; 653-1631

Miya & Miya Employment Agency
4319 Oak Lawn Drive; 521-0500

Moore & Moore Associates
5501 L B J Freeway; 960-1010

Moseley & Associates
13333 N. Central Expressway; 669-1409

New Careers
9645 Covemeadow Road; 691-3411

Norrell Services, Inc.
2001 Bryan Tower; 742-8831

North Dallas Personnel
4455 L B J Freeway; 661-1063

Oak Lawn Personnel Service
5307 Cedar Springs; 559-0490

Odell & Associates
7515 Greenville Avenue; 692-1221

Opportunity Unlimited Professional Placement
2720 W. Mockingbird Lane; 357-9196

Oxford & Associates
10300 N. Central Expressway; 691-3909

Pace Personnel Services
1309 Main Street; 744-0338

Pacific Internat'l Employment Service, Inc.
7110 Dye Street; 931-8090

Pal-Personnel Assistance, Ltd.
558 Hawthorn Road; 424-4077

Palmer-Rockwell
8220 Brookriver Road; 630-9001

Park Personnel Service
Exchange Park Mall; 358-3201

Parkway Recruiters, Inc.
5050 Quorum Drive; 934-0707

Pat Still Personnel Consultants
10822 Stone Canyon Road; 373-6061

Perry White and Associates, Inc.
10300 N. Central Expressway; 263-8411

Personnel Connection
5710 L B J Freeway; 934-1200

Personnel Resources
8616 Northwest Plaza Drive; 361-9123

Petrol Recruiters
10300 N. Central Expressway; 692-5044

Placement Resources
3603 N. Hall Street; 559-0391

Placements, Inc.
9550 Forest Lane; 343-1001

Prestige Placement Services, Inc.
2829 W. Northwest Highway; 353-9950

Preston Personnel Services, Inc.
8226 Douglas Avenue; 363-4331

Priority Placement
11500 Stemmons Freeway; 241-5381

Probe & Associates Personnel Consultants
1111 W. Mockingbird Lane; 638-7020

Productivity Resources, Inc.
5622 Dyer; 739-4135

Professional Employment Consultants
13101 Preston Road; 386-5005

Professional Woman
9144 Chimney Corner; 238-1606

Progressive Personnel Consultants
6060 N. Central Expressway; 739-5140

Quad Employment Agency
5514 Royal Lane; 692-6903

Rainbow Personnel Service
5539 Alpha Road; 458-0755

Retail Associates
12900 Preston Road; 934-2600

Retail Personnel Consultants
417 Lawndale; 231-2281

Retail Recruiters
8300 Douglas Avenue; 691-6585

Retail World
16970 Dallas Parkway; 931-0610

Robert Half and Associates
Two Northpark East; 363-3300

Romac & Associates
6350 L B J Freeway; 980-0606

Rope
1200 Main Street; 741-7673

Roth Young Personnel Service
5344 Alpha Road; 235-5000

Saar Personnel Consultants, Inc.
1507 Pacific Avenue; 744-0061

Sales Finders of America
8700 Stemmons Freeway; 630-0980

Sales World, Inc.
1111 W. Mockingbird Lane; 638-5081

Sanford Rose Associates
2964 L B J Freeway; 247-0136

Search & Associates Personnel Consultants, Inc.
2997 L B J Freeway; 620-8580

Search Employment, Inc.
13773 N. Central Expressway; 783-1018

Search Probe
811 S. Central Expressway; 235-2334

Snelling and Snelling Employment Service
931 Big Town Road; 324-3471

Source EDP
12700 Park Central Plaza; 387-1600

Sumrall Personnel Consultants, Inc.
4101 McEwen; 387-4801

Sur International, Inc.
One Turtle Creek Village; 528-1652

Technical Placements
11300 N. Central Expressway; 373-6036

Technical Recruiters
16935 Park Hill Drive; 980-9940

Town East Employment Service
8035 E R L Thornton; 328-9153

Traver Placement Service
2880 L B J Freeway; 243-2291

VP Personnel, Inc.
100 N. University Drive; 654-2932

Valley View Personnel Service
5710 L B J Freeway; 980-6969

Western Computer Career Consultants
Centre Tower; 980-4090

Worden & Associates
12900 Preston Road; 934-2600

LOS ANGELES

A B C Employment Agency
8383 Wilshire Boulevard; 655-3473

A C Crawford & Co.
704 S. Spring; 629-1693

ACD Personnel Services
2930 W. Imperial Highway; 757-1767

APA Agency
3250 Wilshire Boulevard; 387-2800

A & S Agency
22 W. Valley Boulevard; 254-6751

Abraham & London Ltd. Personnel Service
13440 Ventura Boulevard; 872-0435

Academy Employment Agency
1545 Wilshire Boulevard; 484-2062

Accountants Exchange
5455 Wilshire Boulevard; 933-7411

Accountants Unlimited Personnel Service
8383 Wilshire Boulevard; 852-1166

Accounting Financial Associates
6380 Wilshire Boulevard; 852-1239

Accounting Specialists, Inc.
6363 Wilshire Boulevard; 653-9640

Accurate Personnel Agency
2007 Wilshire Boulevard; 483-0077

Advanced Technology Consultants
6399 Wilshire Boulevard; 852-1539

Alan Howard Associates
16055 Ventura Boulevard; 990-8822

Alhambra Employment Agency
106 S. Chapel Avenue; 283-3691

Allen Alfred & Associates Agency
6151 W. 98th Street; 417-5041

Ambassador Employment Agency
707 S. Broadway; 625-2432

American Personnel Agencies, Inc.
3250 Wilshire Boulevard; 387-2800

Annex Agency
1046 N. Tustin; 639-5151

EMPLOYMENT AGENCIES IN SELECTED MAJOR METROPOLITAN AREAS

Arden Agency
1100 Glendon Avenue; 208-5602

Arno Personnel Service
1115 N. Brand Boulevard; 245-9922

Athena Employment Agency
8447 Wilshire Boulevard; 852-1291

Atlantic-Pacific Personnel Agency
17420 Ventura Boulevard; 872-2073

Atlas Agency
615 S. Flower Street; 627-9611

Atlas Agency
3660 Wilshire Boulevard; 380-8080

B T Bobbitt & Co., Inc.
6118 Venice Boulevard; 937-6770

Bank Personnel Services
205 S. Beverly Drive; 271-2188

Banking Careers Agency
7985 Santa Monica Boulevard; 650-4411

Beedle Associates, Inc.
5301 Laurel Canyon Boulevard; 506-8611

Beeson Agency
1801 Avenue of the Stars; 879-2770

Bell & Associates Agency
3600 Wilshire Boulevard; 385-9091

Benn & Lovick Personnel Service
5701 W. Slauson Avenue; 776-4084

Beverly Cross Agency
1281 Westwood Boulevard; 478-9863

Blaine-Trifon Associates
16055 Ventura Boulevard; 981-9940

Borne & Co.
15300 Ventura Boulevard; 990-9358

Brooks Employment Agency
3660 Wilshire Boulevard; 385-5343

Buck Associates
3142 Wilshire Boulevard; 380-7272

Burdick Employment Systems Agency
6430 W. Sunset Boulevard; 856-0823

Business Management Personnel Agency
3807 Wilshire Boulevard; 386-4630

Businessmen's Clearinghouse Agency
5455 Wilshire Boulevard; 937-0671

Business & Professional Agency
3807 Wilshire Boulevard; 380-8200

Cadillac Associates, Inc.
3255 Wilshire Boulevard; 385-9111

Cannon's Agency
17057 S. Bellflower; 925-9936

Canon Recruiting Systems Agency, Inc.
624 S. Grand Avenue; 623-5981

Career Dimensions Agency
2716 Ocean Park Boulevard; 450-9507

Career Images
2029 Century Park East; 553-5208

Career Management, Inc.
3255 Wilshire Boulevard; 380-1000

Carson-Thomas & Associates Agency
655 S. Hope; 489-4480

Chandler's Employment Agency
3856 W. Santa Barbara Avenue; 299-7000

Collins Recruiters Employment Agency
6311 Yucca; 461-7480

Colonial Agency
11704 Wilshire Boulevard; 879-1930

Colt Systems Agency
1888 Century Park East; 277-4741

Commonwealth Systems Agency
600 S. Commonwealth Avenue; 487-6760

Computer Centre Agency
3807 Wilshire Boulevard; 386-4630

Condor Personnel Service
707 S. Broadway; 624-3911

Corporate Management Consultants
750 E. Green; 449-9444

Coyne & Associates
16055 Ventura Boulevard; 872-1188

Creative Broadcast Services Agency
6290 W. Sunset Boulevard; 467-8151

Data Center Agency
3660 Wilshire Boulevard; 738-7177

Datacon Personnel Services, Inc.
600 S. Commonwealth Avenue; 385-5200

Dinkin & Associates Agency, Inc.
3400 W. 6th; 739-0122

Dominguez Perputo
1401 S. Hope; 744-0377

Don West Agency, Inc.
900 Wilshire Boulevard; 626-5106

APPENDIX II

Dooley & Co. Agency
2040 Avenue of the Stars; 557-0502

Doris Dean Retail Agency
650 S. Grand Avenue; 627-1618

Drake Personnel
10889 Wilshire Boulevard; 385-3576

Dunhill Personnel Service
6404 Wilshire Boulevard; 653-5385

Eagle-One Personnel Service
707 S. Broadway; 628-6421

Ebony Employment Service
5912 S. Central Avenue; 233-8044

Edythe Barnett Employment Agency
156 W. Valley Boulevard; 283-3515

Equitable Agency
1718 Naud Street; 223-3545

**Evans Tiffany & Associates Personnel
  Services**
750 E. Green; 681-4337

Everett Agency
5455 Wilshire Boulevard; 934-5611

Evie Kreisler Agency
110 E. 9th; 622-8994

Execusearch Agency
2007 Wilshire Boulevard; 483-7923

Executive Force Agency
1135 S. Beverly Drive; 557-1300

Executive Opportunities, Inc.
945 S. Prairie Avenue; 673-4635

Executive Recruiting Agency
1901 Avenue of the Stars; 277-8150

F. E. Manning Personnel Services
4554 Sherman Oaks Avenue; 501-4455

Fegan Employment Agency
707 S. Broadway; 623-3764

Financial Careers Agency
3440 Wilshire Boulevard; 384-2122

Fortune Personnel Agency
3440 Wilshire Boulevard; 382-6371

Foster McKay Group Agency
3255 Wilshire Boulevard; 384-4300

Future Personnel Agency
8530 Wilshire Boulevard; 859-2588

Gale Goodwin Personnel Agency
678 S. La Brea Avenue; 938-2111

Galiard Agency
5004 Huntington Drive South; 225-2278

Hallmark Agency
16661 Ventura Boulevard; 981-0340

Haney Systems-Personnel Agency
6404 Wilshire Boulevard; 653-0315

Harmon Associates Agency
3807 Wilshire Boulevard; 738-5023

Hart & Spencer Employment Agency
707 S. Broadway; 627-9823

Harvard Agency, Inc.
3660 Wilshire Boulevard; 739-1200

Harvard Executive Search
3807 Wilshire Boulevard; 387-8947

Heim Lee Agency
707 S. Broadway; 623-4291

Horizons Unlimited Employment Agency
111 E. Broadway; 246-9572

**Howroyd-Wright Employment Agency,
  Inc.**
1250 Westwood Boulevard; 879-9228

Hudson Associates, Inc.
3435 Wilshire Boulevard; 487-1422

Hugh A. Bell & Associates Agency
3600 Wilshire Boulevard; 385-9091

Icon Personnel Agency
830 S. Glendale Avenue; 245-4927

Ideal Personnel Agency
15052 Rosecrans Avenue; 582-1116

Input Search Agency
5670 Wilshire Boulevard; 938-9137

Insurance Placement Agency
3757 Wilshire Boulevard; 385-4306

Insurance Recruitment Agency
3275 Wilshire Boulevard; 386-8850

International Recruiting Systems, Inc.
7100 Hayvenhurst Avenue; 782-0525

International Search Consultants
10100 Santa Monica Boulevard; 553-3888

Jarvis Walker Group Agency
3255 Wilshire Boulevard; 384-4900

Jean Kerr Personnel Service
9521 Las Tunas Drive; 287-5254

Jordan Recruiting & Placement Services
9201 Wilshire Boulevard; 274-0872

Katz Ross & Associates
16255 Ventura Boulevard; 783-7522

Ken Buck Associates Placement Agency
3142 Wilshire Boulevard; 380-7272

Ketchum C. Employment Agency
8185 Seville Avenue; 587-2217

Kingsley Forbes, Ltd.
15910 Ventura Boulevard; 990-9720

Kirksey & Associates
3055 Wilshire Boulevard; 380-0380

LA Financial Agency
5670 Wilshire Boulevard; 938-2716

L & B Associates
110 E. 9th; 624-9804

Lambert Personnel Services
5455 Wilshire Boulevard; 935-5040

Lamco Associates Agency
3660 Wilshire Boulevard; 487-0620

Lance & Associates Agency
3926 Wilshire Boulevard; 385-5111

London Agency
11645 Wilshire Boulevard; 826-6060

Lou Dell Employment Agency
3275 Wilshire Boulevard; 387-2752

Lynn Carol Employment Agency
8500 Wilshire Boulevard; 659-9010

Lynn McIntosh Employment Agency
3807 Wilshire Boulevard; 387-7200

M B C Employment Agency
163 S. Western Avenue; 388-0333

MIT Employment Systems Agency
3440 Wilshire Boulevard; 384-3333

Maggi Nelson Agency
727 W. 7th Street; 626-8791

Management Recruiters
5900 Wilshire Boulevard; 930-1313

Management Register Agency, Inc.
14724 Ventura Boulevard; 990-8000

Manufacturers Service Agency
5670 Wilshire Boulevard; 938-2716

Marc I Enterprises, Inc.
707 S. Broadway Street; 628-6424

Mason Concepts Agency, Inc.
6420 Wilshire Boulevard; 937-0650

McCall & Associates
3600 Wilshire Boulevard; 381-2981

Medley Agency
2029 Century Park East; 552-7892

Merit Personnel Services
3868 W. Carson Street; 772-0604

Milne Agency
3932 Wilshire Boulevard; 385-7194

Mitchell Employment Agency
8615 E. Florence Avenue; 861-9716

Monterey Park Employment Agency
546 E. Garvey Avenue; 283-8049

Nancy Nolan Agency
8383 Wilshire Boulevard; 658-5333

New Concept Personnel Services
5507 S. Central Avenue; 235-5058

Office Overload
121 S. Del Mar Avenue; 266-1105

Ohanesian & Associates
9107 Wilshire Boulevard; 858-8880

Orbit 1 Agency
8022 S. Painter Avenue; 723-1344

Oxford Employment Agency
3926 Wilshire Boulevard; 386-8290

PAT Services, Inc.
2424 W. Sepulveda Boulevard; 775-8031

P S P Personnel, Inc.
3345 Wilshire Boulevard; 385-3991

Pace Personnel Agencies, Inc.
13610 Ventura Boulevard; 788-2755

Pacific Accounting Personnel Agency
3250 Wilshire Boulevard; 380-9091

Pacific Personnel Service
1935 W. Whittier Boulevard; 725-3953

Pacifico Employment Agency
1001 S. Indiana Street; 269-9581

Panorama Employment Agency
14547 Titus Street; 873-1445

Park Avenue Employment Agency
655 S. Hope Street; 623-2282

Perry-White & Associates, Inc.
Two Century Plaza; 552-1700

Preferred Personnel Services
13443 Ventura Boulevard; 872-3743

Presto Employment Agency
2614 W. 8th Street; 381-1636

Pro Select Inc.
1499 Huntington Drive; 799-4112

Professional Management Agency
3255 Wilshire Boulevard; 380-1540

Prompt Employment Services, Inc.
6380 Florence Avenue; 771-5555

Prosearch Recruiters Agency, Inc.
16311 Ventura Boulevard; 995-2900

Provident Personnel Service
3600 Wilshire Boulevard; 384-1159

Purcell Employment Systems
3660 Wilshire Boulevard; 380-4550

Quest Personnel Agency
3450 Wilshire Boulevard; 385-2101

RM Enterprises
6380 Wilshire Boulevard; 651-4622

Ready Personnel
207 E. Pomona Boulevard; 723-2672

Robe Personnel Agency
16055 Ventura Boulevard; 872-3971

Robert Half Personnel Agencies
3600 Wilshire Boulevard; 386-6805

Robertson Agency
1612 W. Glenoaks Boulevard; 245-0952

Roth Young
6133 Bristol Parkway; 670-0521

Royal Personnel Agency
15910 Ventura Boulevard; 872-1124

Rutledge Hunter & Associates
3960 Wilshire Boulevard; 738-1071

Sales Consultants
5901 Green Valley Circle; 670-3040

Sales Consultants Agency
16133 Ventura Boulevard; 986-7550

Sales Development Agency, Inc.
6001 Topanga Canyon Boulevard; 703-7904

Sales Recruiters
16055 Ventura Boulevard; 995-4915

Salesworld, Inc.
10880 Wilshire Boulevard; 475-8601

Sanford Rose Associates
3932 Wilshire Boulevard; 387-5544

Screen Company
10642 Santa Monica Boulevard; 470-2007

Search Unlimited Agency
4827 N. Sepulveda Boulevard; 981-7640

Selected Executives West
3250 Wilshire Boulevard; 385-0443

Shaw & Shaw, Inc.
4825 Torrance Boulevard; 370-8567

Sheldon Marder Agency
8447 Wilshire Boulevard; 655-3520

Sheppard Personnel Employment Agency
8500 Wilshire Boulevard; 854-3555

Silver Search Agency
3400 W. 6th Street; 385-3476

Snelling & Snelling
232 N. Lake Avenue; 449-4610

Source Personnel Services
3550 Wilshire Boulevard; 386-5500

Southland Personnel Services
13540 Ventura Boulevard; 872-3428

Specialized Personnel Agency
5900 Wilshire Boulevard; 933-5861

Squire Employment Agency
99 E. Magnolia Boulevard; 842-9813

Stacom Agency
6290 W. Sunset Boulevard; 856-0817

Star Personnel
23639 Hawthorne Boulevard; 772-5143

Stuart Agency
510 W. 6th Street; 489-2070

Stuart Personnel Services
5855 E. Naples Plaza; 439-0921

Summitt Personnel Agency
211 Beverly Drive; 275-5776

Sunrise Employment Agency
650 S. Grand Avenue; 627-4952

Systematics EDP Agency
3660 Wilshire Boulevard; 487-1020

Talley Personnel Services
5322 Wilshire Boulevard; 857-1231

EMPLOYMENT AGENCIES IN SELECTED MAJOR METROPOLITAN AREAS

Target Employment Agency
4055 Wilshire Boulevard; 381-5691

Thor Agency
4055 Wilshire Boulevard; 487-0130

Timesavers Personnel Services
21150 Hawthorne Boulevard; 373-0501

Tower Personnel Agency
2130 Huntington Drive; 682-3343

21st Century Agency
1901 Avenue of the Stars; 556-1535

U-Gro Agency
8929 Wilshire Boulevard; 855-1454

United California Agency
3325 Wilshire Boulevard; 385-8691

Unlimited Personnel Service, Inc.
13756 Ventura Boulevard; 872-3476

V I P Agency, Inc.
6404 Wilshire Boulevard; 852-0999

Valley Employment Agency
13610 Ventura Boulevard; 872-0008

Vernon Employment Agency
2550 E. Gage Avenue; 583-2245

Volkman Associates, Inc.
9100 Wilshire Boulevard; 273-4785

Weiss & Associates
7033 W. Sunset Boulevard; 465-5172

Wells Recruiting Systems Agency
10100 Santa Monica Boulevard; 553-8090

West Coast Executive Recruiters
21031 Ventura Boulevard; 702-9870

Wolverine Employment Agency
727 W. 7th Street; 626-8794

Appendix III

Executive Recruiters in Selected Major Metropolitan Areas

ATLANTA

Agri-Personnel
5120 Old Bill Cook Road; 768-5701

AID, Inc.
1835 Savoy Drive; 455-7333

American Source
561 Duluth Highway; 962-3735

Atlanta Associates
4651 Roswell Road; 256-6408

Atlanta Management Analysts Systems, Inc.
3480 Greenbriar Parkway; 346-3666

Atlanta Recruiting Corp.
192 Century Boulevard; 633-4173

Baker Lucas & Associates
4501 Harris Street; 266-8413

Banking Group
3035 N. Druid Hills Road; 325-1470

Barton Sans, Inc.
575 Peachtree Center; 588-9723

Beall-Damron, Inc.
2100 Powers Ferry Road; 953-1062

Bell Oaks Consultants
3400 Peachtree Road; 261-2170

Benefield Dotson & Associates, Inc.
2295 Parklake Drive; 493-1441

Bernard Haldane Associates
229 Peachtree Street; 659-3900

Blondi Ray Inc. Executive Search
56 Perimeter Center; 393-8822

Blackshaw And Olmstead, Inc.
134 Peachtree Street; 525-6700

Bob Maddox Associates
3390 Peachtree Road; 231-0558

Boyden Associates, Inc.
3390 Peachtree Road; 261-6532

Career Development Corporation
100 Colony Square; 892-0992

Career Services, Inc.
1819 Peachtree Road; 355-7365

Carter & Overend, Inc.
2045 Peachtree Road; 355-3300

Clark Associates-Industrial
1800 Century Boulevard; 321-3037

Coker Tyler & Co.
1835 Savoy Drive; 451-7991

Compusearch
3300 Buckeye Road; 435-4132

Corporate Personnel, Inc.
4651 Roswell Road; 325-3292

Corporate Search Associates, Inc.
24 Perimeter Park Drive; 455-4163

Don Blouin Associates
3955 Pleasantdale Road; 448-6611

Dunhill of Atlanta, Inc.
3445 Peachtree Road; 261-3751

EDP Search, Inc.
3355 Lenox Road; 262-1210

Elde Peterson Associates, Inc.
5780 Peachtree Dunwoody Road; 256-1661

Execu-Resources
1800 Century Boulevard; 325-7767

Executive Development System
2 Northside 75 Street; 355-8338

Executive Recruiters, Inc.
2895 Whitby Drive; 491-3001

Executive Search
3300 Buckeye Road; 458-4322

Executive Staff Resources
5775 Peachtree Dunwoody Road; 252-7704

Fleming Associates
2625 Cumberland Parkway; 435-2547

Fox & Associates
233 Peachtree Street; 659-4141

Fry Consultants
One Park Place; 352-2293

Futures Unlimited, Inc.
2601 Flowers Road; 455-1133

George & Associates
76 E. Perimeter Center; 396-3895

Gilbert Lane Associates
2840 Mount Wilkinson Parkway; 434-2300

Haskins & Associates
528 Chateaugay Lane; 252-2604

Herman Smith, Inc.
254 E. Paces Ferry Road; 231-1216

Hines Recruiting Associates
3355 Lenox Road; 262-7131

Houchins & Associates, Inc.
250 Piedmont Avenue; 588-0060

I M A G E, Ltd.
2285 Peachtree Road; 351-7777

J Smith Associates
3400 Peachtree Road; 266-1022

Jackson & Coker
4488 Shallowford Road; 393-1210

John William Costello Associates, Inc.
76 Perimeter Center East; 394-7933

Kearney, Inc.
223 Perimeter Center Parkway; 393-9900

Keenum Carman & Associates, Inc.
2300 Henderson Mill Road; 491-8821

Key Career Recruiters
3390 Peachtree Road; 233-1476

Key Search
2971 Flowers Road; 458-7107

Korn-Ferry International
260 Peachtree Street; 577-7542

Lamalie Associates, Inc.
Tower Place; 237-6324

Liberty Associates
2635 Century Parkway; 633-5858

Lovewell & Associates, Inc.
100 Colony Square; 892-8930

M S L International Consultants
1770 The Exchange; 955-9550

MacFarlane & Company, Inc.
One Park Place; 352-2290

Management Centre
One Park Place; 352-2293

Management Recruiters
250 Piedmont Avenue; 588-0060

Management Search, Inc.
Peachtree Center, Harris Tower; 659-5050

McMahon & Associates
5600 Roswell Road; 256-2070

Mills Management, Inc.
2600 Century Parkway; 325-0555

Moley & Associates
2601 S. Flowers Road; 451-8090

Narrin & Associates, Inc.
250 Spring Street; 688-8889

National Executive Consultants, Inc.
1745 Old Spring House; 458-1256

National Executive Search, Inc.
76 Perimeter Center; 394-7931

Noble & Anglin, Inc.
2300 Henderson Mill Road; 491-0056

Omni Executive Search, Inc.
6840 Roswell Road; 394-1200

Opportunities Unlimited, Inc.
229 Peachtree Street; 681-3440

Parker Page of Atlanta
3600 N.E. Expressway; 455-0502

Pettway & Co.
3565 Piedmont Road; 231-0000

Pierce-Catterton, Inc.
233 Peachtree Street; 233-0000

Ray Paul & Co.
3201 Peachtree Street; 892-2727

Retail Recruiters, Inc.
3400 Peachtree Road; 231-9444

Robert Howe & Associates
2971 Flowers Road; 455-6618

Sales Consultants
3300 Buckeye Road; 455-8020

Salesworld, Inc.
2965 S. Flowers Road; 458-8981

Source EDP, Inc.
233 Peachtree Street; 588-9350

Southeastern Associates, Inc.
3390 Peachtree Road; 231-8515

Spectrum Personnel Consultants
3400 Peachtree Road; 231-9444

Status, Inc.
3330 Peachtree Road; 233-8600

Strekus & Associates
4056 Wetherburn Way; 449-1231

Stuart Compton Personnel
4651 Roswell Road; 252-0424

Synergy Resources
3350 Lenox Road; 237-1492

United Consultants of Atlanta
2964 Peachtree Road; 231-3525

Walters & Company
4418 Davidson Avenue; 237-9879

Waterford Inc.
1401 W. Paces Ferry Road; 262-1226

Wells Recruiting Systems
2200 Century Parkway; 321-5425

BOSTON

Aase Associates
1318 Beacon; 738-5000

Aldrich & Associates
176 Second Avenue; 890-5092

American Executive Management
30 Federal Street; 744-5923

Asquith & Jackson Associates, Inc.
586 Boston Post Road; 891-0310

Bailey Employment Service of Needham
10 Kearney Road; 444-5800

Baldwin W. Ray, Jr.
89 Broad Street; 451-0207

Banker's Search of Boston, Inc.
60 State Street; 523-4570

Barry Nathan Associates, Inc.
301 Union Wharf; 227-6067

Bernard Haldane Associates
545 Boylston Street; 437-7110

**Boston Executive Recruitment
  Consultants**
729 Boylston Street; 261-1777

Buffum Associates
2 Center Plaza; 227-4350

Cain & Associates
60 State Street; 367-9540

Canny Bowen, Inc.
39 Harrison Street; 965-0437

Career Dynamics, Inc.
8 Newcomb Road; 662-9636

Charter Associates
89 Broad Street; 451-0207

Consulting Search Associates, Inc.
250 Hammond Pond Parkway; 244-2225

Daly & Company
John Hancock Tower; 262-2800

Data Processing Resource Group
Faneuil Hall Market Place; 367-6983

Davidson Associates, Inc.
594 Marrett Road; 862-0080

Davis & Company
535 Ward; 924-4433

Donahue Associates
176 Second Avenue; 890-3530

Dromeshauser & Graham Associates
886 Washington Street; 329-4200

Dunhill Associates
182 Forbes Road; 848-6320

EDP Direct
751 Main Street; 891-0760

Emerson Personnel, Inc.
Sears Crescent Building; 523-2020

Erwin Stone Associates, Inc.
166 Forbes Road; 848-3040

Executive Careers, Inc.
1020 Statler Building; 426-5300

Executive Sources International
66 Long Wharf; 523-2525

Executives & Understudies, Inc.
11 Newbury Street; 536-1234

Folger & Co., Inc.
214 Lewis Wharf; 227-5900

Gardner and Associates
60 State Street; 720-0270

Garofolo & Co.
66 E. India Row; 227-0260

Grace Associates
745 High Street; 329-0188

Gray & Steele Associates, Inc.
240 Commercial Street; 742-1950

Hammond & Associates
9 Meriam Road; 861-8200

Harrington Associates
148 State Street; 227-1626

Hayden Associates, Inc.
20 Walnut Street; 431-1130

Heath & Co.
19 Judith Road; 527-8839

Heffelfinger Associates, Inc.
888 Washington Street; 329-1040

Heidrick and Struggles, Inc.
100 Federal Street; 423-1140

Ingoldsby Associates, Inc.
62 Derby Street; 749-4080

J K L Associates
50 Milk Street; 542-2490

James Bennett Associates
101 Tremont Street; 357-4453

Keane Associates
329 Beacon Street; 267-2816

Kelley & Associates
60 State Street; 227-2717

Kiernan & Company
1 Washington Street; 742-6330

Kleven & Co., Inc.
181 Bedford Street; 861-1020

Koteen Associates
50 Milk Street; 482-0066

Laiderman Associates, Inc.
36 Washington Street; 235-8336

Lexington Resources Associates, Inc.
594 Marrett Road; 862-2153

Lyell Corporation
145 Pinckney Street; 723-8221

Management Recruiters
607 Boylston Street; 262-5050

Mannix & Co., Inc.
65 William Street; 237-1921

Matte & Company, Inc.
60 State Street; 742-5130

McCusker Associates
Faneuil Hall Market Place; 367-5954

Morton Associates, Inc.
35 Fields Road; 899-4904

Nagler & Co.
60 William Street; 431-1330

Network New England
1330 Beacon Street; 734-5040

Nexus Personnel Services, Inc.
200 W. Cummings Park; 935-8885

Norton Co., Inc.
271 Lincoln Street; 861-7800

O R I Organization Resources, Inc.
63 Atlantic Avenue; 742-8970

Option 2, Inc.
131 Clarendon Street; 266-9620

Par Associates, Inc.
27 State Street; 367-0320

Parker Eldridge Sholl & Gordon
440 Totten Road; 890-0340

Pencarski Co., Inc.
850 Providence Highway; 329-5430

Perry-White & Associates, Inc.
300 Bear Hill Road; 890-6500

Pilgrim Personnel
120 Boylston Street; 482-9732

Prime Selection, Inc.
28 Edgehill Road; 894-9360

Promotions Co.
1 Center Plaza; 227-7722

Quest Associates
235 W. Central Avenue; 237-2030

Rando Associates
274 Main Street; 944-0990

Reliance National
129 Newbury Street; 266-1553

Retail Recruiters
850 Providence Highway; 329-5850

Richards Consultants
131 State Street; 227-1977

Rudzinsky Associates
1656 Massachusetts Avenue; 862-6727

Russillo and Associates
60 State Street; 720-1113

Sales Consultants of Boston, Inc.
155 Middlesex Turnpike; 273-1430

Salesworld, Inc.
460 Totten Pond Road; 890-1500

Sampson Associates, Inc.
50 Milk Street; 482-4588

Sandel Associates
479 Winter Street; 890-0713

Selected Executives, Inc.
959 Park Square; 426-3100

Smallhorn Executive Recruiting, Inc.
55 Kilby Street; 482-1899

Source EDP
45 William Street; 237-3120

Staples Associates
3 N.E. Executive Park; 272-8910

Stepan & Co.
73 Tremont Street; 742-2772

Stevenson Group, Inc.
66 Long Wharf; 367-3675

Studwell Associates of Boston
6 Faneuil Hall Market Place; 367-3669

Telesearch, Inc.
310 Washington Street; 237-6591

Thorne Associates
2 Newton Executive Park; 969-1810

Trans World Recruitment Specialists
10 Tremont Street; 723-7874

Universal Management Associates
6 Faneuil Hall Market Place; 367-1110

Windsor Greene Associates
545 Boylston Street; 267-6505

Wright Companies
53 Main Street; 369-7354

Zabriskie Associates, Inc.
2366 Commonwealth Avenue; 899-5511

CHICAGO

Accountants Amdo
55 E. Monroe Street; 726-4591

Accountants Center Ltd.
7 W. Madison Avenue; 782-3960

Accountants Professional Staff, Inc.
25 E. Washington Street; 263-5070

Accounting Association, Inc.
6 N. Michigan Avenue; 332-6722

Accu-Executive Search
1211 W. 22nd Oak Street; 242-1080

Administrative Resources
188 Industrial Drive; 626-6310

Administrative Search Associates
209 W. Jackson Boulevard; 435-1111

American Data Consultants
5234 W. Diversy Street; 286-6903

American Personnel Consultants, Inc.
30 W. Washington Street; 263-6463

Ams Search, Ltd.
2 N. LaSalle Street; 372-1525

Argus Associates, Inc.
29 S. LaSalle Street; 853-0875

Ashton & Associates
999 Plaza Drive; 843-7788

Avid Execu-Search
2720 River Road; 694-2884

Baker-Hulce Associates, Inc.
625 N. Michigan Avenue; 280-9317

Bankers Group
120 S. Riverside; 930-1111

Bankers Personnel Service
11 S. LaSalle Street; 332-7190

Banner Personnel
7 W. Madison Avenue; 641-6456

Barnett-Fulson & Associates
625 N. Michigan Avenue; 664-3818

Behro Associates
7 W. Madison Avenue; 641-6667

Bertrand Ross & Associates, Inc.
216 Higgins Road; 698-2300

Blecha Cohen Tokarz & Associates, Inc.
7330 N. Cicero; 677-7000

Boyden Associates, Inc.
10 S. Riverside; 782-1581

Burkett & Associates Inc.
1010 Jorie Boulevard; 920-1770

Business Careers, Inc.
444 N. Michigan Avenue; 664-8166

C & C Inc.
20 N. Wacker Drive; 853-0040

Cemco, Ltd.
233 S. Wacker Drive; 876-1700

C F F & Associates, Inc.
9400 W. Foster Street; 992-2382

CHS & Associates
4747 W. Peterson Street; 725-6001

CRT Search
8 S. Michigan Avenue; 781-0190

Cadillac Associates, Inc.
32 W. Randolph Street; 346-9400

Career Specialist, Inc.
800 Main Street; 395-8140

Carroll Associates
150 N. Wacker Drive; 263-5041

Catch & Associates
20 N. Wacker Drive; 346-9295

Central Clearing Inc.
7034 W. North Street; 637-2700

Challenger Gray & Christmas, Inc.
11 S. LaSalle Street; 332-5790

Charles Stuart Group
150 N. Wacker Drive; 641-1646

Clark Associates, Inc.
200 E. Randolph Street; 565-1300

Clayton Group, Inc.
360 N. Michigan Avenue; 558-1063

Compu-Kore, Inc.
150 S. Wacker Drive; 782-1024

Compupro
55 W. Monroe Street; 263-5507

Compusearch, Inc.
6400 Schafer Court; 692-6510

Computer Intelligence Group
25 E. Washington Street; 263-3828

Compass Sentrex, Inc.
2000 Spring Road; 655-4888

Computer Services
4413 W. Roosevelt Road; 449-2040

Concept Corp.
625 N. Michigan Avenue; 280-1717

Conley Associates, Inc.
135 S. LaSalle Street, 263-4680

Consultant Services, Inc.
7330 N. Cicero; 677-7000

Cook Associates, Inc.
35 E. Wacker Drive; 263-1119

Cox & Associates, Inc.
410 N. Michigan Avenue; 644-2360

Cybertek Management Services
208 S. LaSalle Street; 782-3941

Data Interactions
410 N. Michigan Avenue; 527-0410

Data Processing Recruiters
17 W. 727G Butterfield Road; 629-8690

Data Management Search
222 W. Adams Street; 443-1077

Delta Consulting & Search Group
8 S. Michigan Avenue; 346-7808

Dickson Engineering Services
36 S. State Street; 346-9480

Directed Research, Inc.
535 N. Michigan Avenue; 664-8250

Duffy, Inc.
1609 Sherman Avenue; 328-7977

Dunhill of Chicago, Inc.
180 N. Michigan Avenue; 346-0933

Dzierzynski & Associates
230 N. Michigan Avenue; 346-4370

Eastman & Beaudine, Inc.
111 W. Monroe Street; 726-8195

Edwards & Sowers Inc.
875 N. Michigan Avenue; 266-1100

Edwards Swanston & Fox
55 E. Jackson Boulevard; 786-1820

Egon Zehnder International, Inc.
One First National Plaza; 782-4500

Esq Personnel Service, Inc.
180 N. Michigan Avenue; 346-6800

Executive Assets Corp.
111 E. Wacker Drive; 467-0476

Executive Search Group
596 Green Bay Road; 441-8760

Fee Associates, Inc.
20 N. Wacker Drive; 372-0400

Field Engineering Enterprises
360 N. Michigan Avenue; 726-1666

Finney & Associates, Inc.
800 W. Central Road; 577-2090

First Midwestern Service, Inc.
30 N. LaSalle Street; 443-1470

Fortune Personnel of Chicago
500 N. Michigan Avenue; 467-9130

Foster & Associates, Inc.
111 E. Wacker Drive; 861-0030

Fulline Systems, Inc.
4413 W. Roosevelt Road; 449-5510

Gaffney & Associates
500 Park Boulevard; 980-5500

Gillick Ridenour & Associates, Ltd.
221 N. LaSalle Street; 236-4666

Glickauf Daniel & Associates
2 N. Riverside Plaza; 454-0099

Goetz & Associates
14 E. Jackson Boulevard; 786-1641

Greenwood & Associates
35 E. Wacker Drive; 236-5040

Hallmark Associates, Inc.
333 N. Michigan Avenue; 263-3101

Hegarty & Company
875 N. Michigan Avenue; 944-3400

Heidrick & Struggles
125 S. Wacker Drive; 372-8811

Heidrick Associates, Inc.
20 N. Wacker Drive; 726-2777

Hersher Associates, Ltd.
15 Pine Street; 945-5907

Heuristics, Inc.
228 N. LaSalle Street; 346-8808

Hinman W. Warner & Co.
875 N. Michigan Avenue; 951-8010

Hirtz & Associates, Inc.
150 N. Wacker Drive; 977-1555

Hite Co.
104 S. Michigan Avenue; 726-3732

Holland, Inc.
625 N. Michigan Avenue; 649-0903

Houze Shourds & Montgomery, Inc.
3 First National Plaza; 332-4488

Howard Personnel
500 N. Michigan Avenue; 222-1980

Human Resource Developers, Inc.
112 W. Oak Street; 644-1920

Ims Corp.
188 W. Randolph Street; 977-0700

Imber Associates
1821 Wolden Office Square; 397-3090

Interface Associates
16 W. Erie Street; 337-0206

International Management Services, Inc.
216 Higgins Road; 698-0206

Interviewing Dynamics
444 N. Michigan Avenue; 836-1200

Intromation, Inc.
800 Enterprise Street; 654-4288

Itex Executive Search
6400 Shafer Court; 299-2000

J. L. Russell Consultants
836 S. Northwest Highway; 382-2640

JMB Financial Services
205 W. Wacker Drive; 263-1960

Johnson & Genrich, Inc.
5481 N. Milwaukee; 792-2323

Johnson & Associates, Inc.
332 S. Michigan Avenue; 663-4176

Johnson Rankin & Associates
100 W. Monroe Street; 372-0125

Justin Strom & Associates
7330 N. Cicero; 677-7000

Judd Falk, Inc.
One Illinois Center; 856-1400

Keith Ross & Associates, Inc.
150 N. Wacker Drive; 558-1850

Kemper Associates
200 W. Monroe Street; 346-3914

Kennedy Associates, Inc.
520 N. Michigan Avenue; 828-9474

Kerbee King & Associates
2 N. Riverside Plaza; 454-1552

Kilmer & Associates
6149 N. Talman Street; 761-4757

Korn-Ferry International
120 S. Riverside Plaza; 726-1841

Kunzer Associates, Ltd.
208 S. LaSalle Street; 641-0010

Lamson Griffiths Associates
20 N. Wacker Drive; 332-4571

Lauer Sbarbaro Associates, Inc.
1 N. LaSalle Street; 372-7050

Ledger Associates, Inc.
1018 W. Bryon; 327-3737

Lee & Paulin Associates
55 W. Monroe Street; 236-5026

Lockman & Associates, Inc.
2700 River Road; 694-2380

M I S, Inc.
327 S. LaSalle Street; 939-7676

M W Search, Inc.
29 E. Madison Avenue; 781-0070

Management Information Search
327 S. LaSalle Street; 939-7676

**Management Professional Specialist
   International**
30 N. Michigan Avenue; 641-3160

Management Recruiters
4256 N. Arlington Heights Road; 577-9800

Management World
7200 N. Ridge Road; 274-1608

Marr, Inc.
106 Wilmot Road; 948-5160

Martin Zwahlen & Associates, Inc.
20 N. Wacker Drive; 332-3666

Masters Associates
200 W. Monroe Street; 332-0444

McCoy & Associates, Inc.
55 E. Washington Street; 726-3221

McGarrh Search
701 Lee Street; 298-4103

McSherry & Associates
307 N. Michigan Avenue; 332-1333

Mendheim Co.
6055 N. Lincoln Street; 973-6969

Menzel Robinson Baldwin, Inc.
550 W. Campus Drive; 394-4303

Metro Search, Inc.
79 W. Monroe Street; 782-6804

Middle Management Search, Inc.
1935 N. Shermer Road; 272-5915

Moore & Associates
35 E. Wacker Drive; 853-0150

Moriarty-Fox, Inc.
20 N. Wacker Drive; 332-4600

Nadler Group, Inc.
120 W. Madison Avenue; 621-0020

National Executive Search
701 N. Michigan Avenue; 664-1800

National Executive Search, Inc.
30 N. LaSalle Street; 236-1130

National Metal Services Corp.
2711 W. 183rd; 799-3510

National Recruiters
4908 N. Lincoln Avenue; 271-0200

Norris & Associates
6 N. Michigan Avenue; 236-5917

O'Connor & Associates
327 S. LaSalle Street; 939-1392

O'Neill & Associates, Inc.
11 E. Adams Street; 663-1650

Orne & Associates
333 E. Ontario; 944-1013

Ott & Associates
20 N. Wacker Drive; 236-8008

Pabst & Associates
205 W. Wacker Drive; 263-1960

**Pahlman Murphy & Attridge Employment
   Specialists**
180 N. Michigan Avenue; 236-9036

Parenti & Jacobs, Inc.
115 S. LaSalle Street; 782-9844

Petersen Enterprise
55 E. Washington Street; 332-5444

Phillip Graham Associates, Ltd.
845 N. Michigan Avenue; 951-5757

Phillips & Associates, Inc.
166 E. Superior Street; 266-8529

Phoenix Systems, Inc.
625 N. Michigan Avenue; 664-0934

Pinkerton & Associates
625 N. Michigan Avenue; 266-8669

Plaza, Inc.
55 E. Monroe Street; 263-0944

Polsky Associates
20 N. Clark Street; 782-1450

Poulos Associates
1139 Scott Street; 446-5494

Priority 1, Ltd.
327 S. LaSalle Street; 939-5562

Pro-Search, Inc.
3256 Ridge Road; 895-8800

Professional Executive Consultants
3000 Dundee Road; 564-3900

Professional Support Personnel
185 N. Wabash Street; 236-8787

Pyramid Search, Inc.
2400 E. Devon Street; 694-3757

R W Consultants
625 N. Michigan Avenue; 751-0713

Ray & Company, Inc.
100 S. Wacker Drive; 876-0730

Ray White Associates
875 N. Michigan Avenue; 266-0100

Rezek & Associates
314 W. Arlington Heights Road; 577-9790

Right Associates
332 S. Michigan Avenue; 663-4179

Robert Half of Chicago, Inc.
35 E. Wacker Drive; 782-6930

Robert Heidrick Associates, Inc.
20 N. Wacker Drive; 726-2777

Robertson Molidor & Wengert
120 S. Riverside Plaza; 930-1958

Roth Young Personnel Service
444 N. Michigan Avenue; 222-1818

Russell Reynolds Associates, Inc.
200 S. Wacker Drive; 993-9696

S R S Data Search
6 N. Michigan Avenue; 346-6383

Sales Consultants
303 E. Wacker Drive; 922-7855

Sales Executives, Inc.
8420 Bryn Mawr; 693-0090

Sales & Management Search, Inc.
120 S. Riverside Plaza; 930-1111

Salesworld, Inc.
9801 W. Higgins Road; 692-9000

Search Enterprises, Inc.
2122 York Road; 654-1022

Search Group
2 Northfield Plaza; 446-6460

Search Systems, Ltd.
1701 E. Woodfield Drive; 843-8282

Securities Resource Management
200 W. Monroe Street; 346-2155

Sells & Company, Inc.
Two Illinois Center; 565-1252

Shamrock Consultants
9701 Higgins Road; 692-4300

Smith & Co., Inc.
221 N. LaSalle Street; 726-3132

Spencer Stuart & Associates
500 N. Michigan Avenue; 822-0080

Stafford Associates, Ltd.
222 S. Riverside Plaza; 454-0942

Stehlik Dennis Associates, Inc.
1211 W. 22nd Oak Street; 655-0600

Studwell & Associates
112 S. Grant Place; 655-2550

Sudlow & Co.
625 N. Michigan Avenue; 944-5127

Synergistics Associates
875 N. Michigan Avenue; 337-4650

Technical Recruiting System
836 S. Northwest Highway; 382-1500

Technology Associates, Inc.
535 N. Michigan Avenue; 467-1811

Thomas & Associates, Inc.
2315 E. 103 Street; 731-7800

Thompson & Associates
55 E. Washington Street; 263-0335

Transactor Systems, Inc.
500 N. Michigan Avenue; 822-0333

Transactor Systems, Inc.
1620 N. Wells Street; 951-0868

Ultra-Search Associates, Inc.
179 W. Washington Street; 346-9445

United Executives, Ltd.
2720 S. Des Plaines Avenue; 297-5155

Vaughan & Associates, Inc.
8 S. Michigan Avenue; 346-7428

Verkanp-Joyce Associates, Inc.
616 Enterprise Drive; 920-1104

Wade Sandy Company
646 N. Michigan Avenue; 280-9036

Ward Howell International Inc.
875 N. Michigan Avenue; 266-9431

Wells Recruiting Systems Loop, Inc.
300 W. Washington Street; 236-6999

Wesley Brown, Ltd.
645 N. Michigan Avenue; 440-0776

Wilkins and Company, Inc.
233 S. Wacker Drive; 930-1036

Williams Roth Krueger, Inc.
101 N. Wacker Drive; 977-0800

Womack Scoglio & Associates
919 N. Michigan Avenue; 951-6003

Wood Computer Associates
35 E. Wacker Drive; 726-6220

Wytmar & Company
10 S. Riverside Plaza; 236-1350

Young & Company
One IBM Plaza; 751-3030

Zehnder Egon International, Inc.
One First National Plaza; 782-4500

DALLAS

ALF Employment Agency
2655 Villa Creek Drive; 243-2374

Abrams Warrick & Winstead
9850 N. Central Expressway; 696-3772

Accounting Personnel Consultants
14114 Dallas Parkway; 386-4770

Accounting Resources International
3131 Turtle Creek Boulevard; 559-3260

Alderson Associates
11500 Stemmons Freeway; 247-1636

American Data Probe
210 S. Main Street; 298-4912

Associated Resources
12201 Merit; 233-9842

Banker's Confidential Referral Service
5580 L B J Freeway; 387-4510

**Barker Financial Management
Corporation**
6350 L B J Freeway; 980-8403

Bent Tree Executive Search
16475 Dallas Parkway; 931-2325

Billington Fox & Ellis
One Main Plaza; 744-4900

Brennan Associates
4101 McEwen; 980-0779

Brooks Brownsted & Associates
5757 Alpha Road; 387-3300

Bryant Bureau Recruiting Services
2225 E. Randolph Mill Road; 261-3331

Byrd International, Inc.
1111 W. Mockingbird Lane; 630-4000

Career-Management Consultants
1309 Main Street; 651-1913

Carter & Associates, Inc.
First Bank & Trust Building; 234-3296

Carter Johnson Associates
301 Loop 820; 589-0803

Catterton, Inc.
6730 L B J Freeway; 934-9000

Computer Careers
4101 McEwen; 387-4010

Computer Logistics, Inc.
2829 W. Northwest Highway; 350-0000

Concept Insearch
11325 Pegasus; 341-6651

Corporate Advisors, Inc.
5580 L B J Freeway; 386-8641

Costello & Associates, Inc.
8585 Stemmons Freeway; 630-7043

Crown Agency
3003 L B J Freeway; 247-4994

Daniel & Associates, Inc.
4230 L B J Freeway; 239-0955

Dunhill of Dallas, Inc.
13101 Preston Road; 661-9494

Dynamix of Dallas
6001 Skillman Road; 739-6160

E D P Southwest
2995 L B J Freeway; 243-8844

Emmons-Labus & Associates, Inc.
4455 L B J Freeway; 661-0163

Energy Personnel Corp.
16935 Park Hill; 931-1778

Etheridge & Associates, Inc.
2655 Villa Creek Drive; 241-2145

Executive Resources Search Consultants
8350 Meadow Road; 361-8972

Executive Search Professionals
5952 Royal Lane; 369-5161

Executive World, Inc.
9400 N. Central Expressway; 691-6900

Fand-Green Associates
12201 Merit Street; 934-2318

Favro Richard Associates
1115 Timplemore Road; 750-8400

First Main Associates
8700 King George; 634-2860

Foresight Services
7616 L B J Freeway; 661-8384

Furst Executive Selection, Ltd.
5726 L B J Freeway; 980-7360

Gorham & Co.
3764 Royal Lane; 350-7316

Group Dynamics, Inc.
4560 Belt Line Road; 233-9284

Hilbert Corporation
14114 Dallas Parkway; 386-4770

Hunter Group
8700 King George; 631-5965

Hurst & Associates, Inc.
Citizens Bank Center; 231-5075

Hyde-Danforth-Lenderman & Co.
1145 Empire Central Place; 630-1866

Hyman MacKenzie & Partners, Inc.
100 N. Central Expressway; 644-6601

In Sync International
3131 Turtle Creek Boulevard; 528-2111

Insurance Search International
500 S. Ervay; 742-3748

International Search
1200 Main Street; 741-7372

Johnson & Associates
2200 Camp David; 285-6410

Jordan Associates
5728 L B J Freeway; 385-8251

Kenzer Corp.
8200 Brookriver; 638-1777

Korn-Ferry International
One Dallas Centre; 651-1801

LSM Associates
5710 L B J Freeway; 934-1444

Lamalie Associates, Inc.
First International Building; 747-1994

Largent Parks & Partners, Inc.
Carillon Tower East; 980-0047

LeMiles Winson and Co.
8563 Manderville; 750-5800

Lineback Associates
Campbell Centre; 750-7250

Livingston Price, Inc.
2403 Skyview; 783-1486

MRA Associates
Executive Towers; 647-0077

Management Recruiters of Dallas
8350 N. Central Expressway; 373-8022

Managerial Women
Ridglea Bank Building; 429-9620

Manor & Associates, Inc.
14110 Dallas Parkway; 387-2235

Martin Harris and Associates, Inc.
7515 Greenville Avenue; 691-3430

McKeen & Co.
Addison State Bank Building; 233-8007

Micarelli & Co.
4455 L B J Freeway; 934-8099

Miller Personnel Services, Inc.
333 W. Campbell Road; 231-5306

Monty & Associates
2925 L B J Freeway; 484-4185

National Executive Search, Inc.
8585 Stemmons Freeway; 630-7041

Oxford Search, Inc.
50 D Business Parkway; 669-1313

Patt Walker Associates, Inc.
8235 Douglas Avenue; 263-1165

Personnel Resources
8616 Northwest Plaza Drive; 361-9123

Petro Search of Dallas
5952 Royal Lane; 361-9032

Pool Henry & Partners
3131 Turtle Creek Boulevard; 522-6010

Productivity Resources, Inc.
5622 Dyer; 739-4135

Professional Career Consultants
13612 Midway; 661-9230

Professional Employment Consultants
13101 Preston Road; 386-5005

Professional Woman
9144 Chimney Corner; 238-1606

R V Associates
6060 N. Central Expressway; 369-4225

Raleigh & Company
13101 Preston Road; 386-4685

Rath & Strong System Product, Inc.
4835 L B J Freeway; 980-0647

Ray & Company, Inc.
Plaza Of The Americas; 651-9812

Risk & Benefit Recruiters
3131 Turtle Creek Boulevard; 559-3820

Rogers & Associates
10300 N. Central Expressway; 739-1382

Rope
1200 Main Street; 741-7673

Sadovsky & Associates
12700 Park Central Place; 387-8580

Sampson Associates
717 N. Harwood Street; 749-0330

Sea-Scan
2775 Villa Creek Drive; 620-0147

Search America Personnel Consultants
12700 Hillcrest Road; 233-3302

Search Probe
811 S. Central Expressway; 235-2334

Search Systems, Inc.
14114 Dallas Parkway; 980-0366

Shisler Wicks & Associates
5580 L B J Freeway; 387-8656

Simpson & Associates
4020 McEwen; 980-0011

Snelling and Snelling Employment Service
8350 N. Central Expressway; 363-8800

Source Personnel
12700 Park Central Place; 387-1600

Spencer & Associates
Republic National Bank Tower; 748-1990

Streater & Co.
530 Bedford Road; 268-6484

Sumrall Personnel Consultants, Inc.
4101 McEwen; 387-4801

Swanstrom & Associates
One North Park East; 363-5597

Technical Recruiters
16935 Park Hill; 980-9940

Trotman Wheat & Associates
12201 Merit; 386-8888

White Associates
6060 N. Central Expressway; 750-7348

Winburne & Associates
5501 L B J Freeway; 960-1758

LOS ANGELES

A & L Executive Search
11140 Los Alamitos Boulevard; 594-6977

Aames Executive & Medical Search
9570 Wilshire Boulevard; 271-6164

Abbott Johnson & Rogers
3807 Wilshire Boulevard; 387-9422

Academy Employment Agency
1545 Wilshire Boulevard; 484-2062

Accountants Rescue
700 S. Flower Street; 680-3550

Accounting Resources International
500 Newport Center Drive; 625-0781

Advanced Technology Consultants
6399 Wilshire Boulevard; 852-1539

Alan Howard Associates
16055 Ventura Boulevard; 990-8822

Albright Associates
3807 Wilshire Boulevard; 387-9651

Altschuler Co.
120 S. Reno; 380-1270

Anderson Izzi & Co.
10642 Santa Monica Boulevard; 475-7621

Arnett-Gabriel & Associates, Inc.
6151 W. Century Boulevard; 645-0180

B T Bobbitt & Co., Inc.
6118 Venice Boulevard; 937-6770

Billington & Associates
3250 Wilshire Boulevard; 386-7511

Billington Fox & Ellis
3701 Wilshire Boulevard; 386-4700

Boyden Associates, Inc.
5670 Wilshire Boulevard; 933-5563

Business & Professional Consultants
3807 Wilshire Boulevard; 387-8331

Cadillac Associates, Inc.
3255 Wilshire Boulevard; 385-9111

Canon Recruiting Systems Agency, Inc.
624 S. Grand Avenue; 623-5981

Career Management, Inc.
3255 Wilshire Boulevard; 380-1000

Careers for Women
9911 W. Pico Boulevard; 277-7754

Carre-Orban & Partners
555 S. Flower; 489-2240

Commonwealth Systems Agency
600 S. Commonwealth Avenue; 487-6760

Data-Search
3807 Wilshire Boulevard; 387-9331

Datacon Personnel Services, Inc.
600 S. Commonwealth Avenue; 385-8533

de Meriler Reynolds Rettig Incorporated
617 S. Olive Street; 689-9600

Diogenes Group
617 S. Olive Street; 623-4567

Eastman & Beaudine, Inc.
2049 Century Park East; 552-6005

Execudex West Los Angeles, Inc.
9841 Airport Boulevard; 776-7343

Executive Recruiting Agency
1901 Avenue of the Stars; 277-8150

Fein & Associates
6733 Sepulveda Boulevard; 649-5250

Fiore & Associates
915 S. Serrano Avenue; 738-8793

First Technical Services
10709 Venice Boulevard; 204-2644

Forty Plus of Southern California
3750 W. 6th Street; 388-2301

Gibson Associates, Inc.
5900 Wilshire Boulevard; 930-1100

Gordon Associates
1528 N. Curson Avenue; 874-2478

Haldane Associates
3807 Wilshire Boulevard; 387-3311

Heidrick and Struggles, Inc.
445 S. Figueroa; 624-8891

Hergenrather & Company
3435 Wilshire Boulevard; 385-0181

Hilton Search
8455 Beverly Boulevard; 655-5150

Horizon Associates
205 Avenue I; 540-3231

Houck Meng & Co.
6151 W. Century Boulevard; 641-8145

Houze Shourds & Montgomery, Inc.
2029 Century Park East; 552-6027

Hudson Associates, Inc.
3435 Wilshire Boulevard; 487-1422

Hugh A. Bell & Associates Agency
3600 Wilshire Boulevard; 385-9091

Hunt & Associates
900 Wilshire Boulevard; 489-7200

Independent Search Consultants
6515 W. Sunset Boulevard; 856-0088

Input Search Agency
5670 Wilshire Boulevard; 938-9137

Keith Management Co.
170 S. Beverly Drive; 274-8664

Kelley Dixon Associates, Inc.
515 S. Flower Street; 624-5540

Kerr Personnel Service
700 S. Flower Street; 627-2808

Koenigsberg & Udell
1900 Avenue of the Stars; 552-3133

Korn-Ferry International
1900 Avenue of the Stars; 879-1634

Kremple & Meade
1900 Avenue of the Stars; 553-3156

Lambert Personnel Services
5455 Wilshire Boulevard; 935-5040

Line Management Co.
1888 Century Park East; 552-2009

Malsin Seymour
1888 Century Park East; 556-0372

Management Recruiters of Southern California
5900 Wilshire Boulevard; 930-1313

Management & Technical Services
8200 Wilshire Boulevard; 655-9230·

Mason Concepts Agency, Inc.
6420 Wilshire Boulevard; 937-0650

McCall & Associates
3600 Wilshire Boulevard; 381-2981

National Executive Search
1801 Avenue of the Stars; 277-7973

Odessa Group
Pacific Mutual Life Building; 629-9181

Paul Norsell & Associates, Inc.
9841 Airport Boulevard; 776-7343

Peterson and Co.
1801 Avenue of the Stars; 277-3711

Philip Lawrence Associates
110 E. 9th Street; 489-4110

Professional Management Agency
3255 Wilshire Boulevard; 380-1540

Purcell Employment Systems
3660 Wilshire Boulevard; 380-4550

Regal Assistance
1930 Wilshire Boulevard; 413-4831

Russell Reynolds Associates, Inc.
555 S. Flower Street; 489-1520

Satcom Association
6290 W. Sunset Boulevard; 856-0818

Search International
1801 Avenue of the Stars; 879-9116

Selected Executives West
3250 Wilshire Boulevard; 385-0443

Shiplacoff & Associates
1801 Avenue of the Stars; 557-3080

Specialized Personnel Agency
5900 Wilshire Boulevard; 933-5861

Spencer Stuart & Associates
523 W. 6th Street; 620-0814

Stacom Association
6290 W. Sunset Boulevard; 856-0816

Streeter-Fricke & Associates
3250 Wilshire Boulevard; 480-1022

Thomas Mangum Co.
1145 W. 6th Street; 977-0600

VIP Agency, Inc.
6404 Wilshire Boulevard; 852-0999

Varhill Associates
445 S. Figueroa; 489-7135

Varo and Lund Corp.
1800 N. Highland Avenue; 469-3109

Wilder & Associates
8455 Beverly Boulevard; 655-2979

4